DREAMS   AND   OMENS

FOULSHAM'S "NEW" POPULAR HANDBOOKS

DREAMS & OMENS

JAMES WARD

REVISED AND ENLARGED
EDITION

LONDON
W. FOULSHAM & CO., LTD.,
NEW YORK . TORONTO . CAPE TOWN . SYDNEY

W. FOULSHAM & CO. LTD.

Yeovil Road, Slough, Berks., England.

572 00163 0

PRINTED IN GREAT BRITAIN BY
ST EDMUNDSBURY PRESS, BURY ST EDMUNDS, SUFFOLK
© W. FOULSHAM & CO., LTD.

CONTENTS

DREAMS AND OMENS

SECTION I

DREAMS AND VISIONS

To many people, there are two worlds—the one in which they live daily, and the one into which they appear to enter on going to sleep, and in many cases, the one state seems as real to them as the other.

> " We are such stuff
> as dreams are made of ; and our little life
> is rounded with a sleep."
>
> " The Tempest " (SHAKESPEARE).

From time immemorial in the history of all nations, dreams and their meanings have been regarded with a wonder and interest transcending mere superstition ; indeed, far from being looked upon only as idle fancies, they have been studied for thousands of years by scientists, as a subject worthy of their attention and investigation, both as to their cause and their meaning. Psychologists and professors of both Eastern and Western worlds have amassed a large amount of evidence on which to work, and the result of their study and deductions would fill many volumes.

Dreams come to everyone at some time or other, even indeed to animals. Who has not heard a dog, while lying asleep before the fire, whine and whimper in its sleep, or watched the family cat twitch and bristle from ears to tail, as it dreams of things unknown to us.

To humans, sometimes, dreams are of so vivid a nature that it is not surprising that they make an impression on the mind strong enough to be remembered in the waking world, and so real do these dreams events seem, that on

7

awaking, it is almost impossible to realise that the experiences dreamed of have not been actually undergone.

The Cause of Dreams

What makes us dream ? Roughly, the cause may be divided into two classes. Dreams may be caused by reflex action of the brain cells, impressions made during the day being distorted, or are imprinted so strongly on the mind that even in sleep the events are lived through again. Jumbled dreams with confused sights and sounds can be usually attributed to direct physical causes, fatigue, indigestion, or shock, and these can be dismissed as not coming within the scope of " message " dreams or visions.

It is the dreams that seem sequential and straightforward that are to be regarded as being direct messages ; and which have led people to believe that such dreams have their fixed laws, and that the dreaming state may be an extension of existence, governed by special conditions, though different in character from those of the waking state, and with which opinion many psychologists concur.

Professor Freud, one of the most famous authorities on this subject, believed that these dreams were the fulfilment of wishes latent beneath our consciousness, and that these wishes showed what the dreamer most desired to attain when he awoke. Freud divided dreams therefore also into two classes, latent dreams, or personal desires, which might or might not be granted in the dream ; and manifest dreams, those in which the dreamer either witnessed or participated in the actions. These are what one might call the real " message " dream or visions. In these the dreamer himself may undergo the events, foreshadowing what may be about to transpire in the future, or he may be only an observer of the drama that is unfolded before his eyes, the events being possibly a warning of experiences to come, or only pictures of events that have already taken place. Such dreams have been held always to be caused by outside and supernatural influences.

The Antiquity of Dream Interpretations

The antiquity in the belief of dreams is age-old. However far back we refer in the history of countries, we find that dreams were treated as direct messages from divine beings, and held in awe and reverence accordingly. The primitive races made dreams play a very prominent part in their religious rites, and the priestcraft of all nations have always played upon the superstitions of the people. The main bulk of them were encouraged by the priests to bring their dreams to them to be interpreted. Dream books were also compiled, and we have records made even in early Siamese history of such documents.

The Greeks believed firmly in dreams and omens, and although they grew to recognise that their gods and goddesses whom they worshipped, no longer came down to earth from their Heaven they termed Olympus, yet they did believe that their commands were issued to mortals through the mouthpieces of priests and priestesses at special temples called oracles, and that Zeus, the Father of the Gods, sent them by means of dreams in the care of his messenger Hermes (in Latin, Mercury). Amongst the lesser gods were Hypnos (Sleep), Oneiros (Dreams), and Thanatos (Death). The " messages " were often given at shrines or oracles dedicated to the different gods, one of the most famous being that of Apollo, at Delphi. Here the priestess would fall into a trance or " sleep," in which the message would be revealed to the devotee. Many took advantage to sleep in the temple, and obtain their own answer to their prayers, and sometimes, when the answer came by word of mouth from the oracle, the answer would be in a cryptic form so that whatever really happened in the future, the oracle had yet spoken truly. Here are a few instances. Croesus consulted the Delphic oracle before setting forth on his journey. He was told that, " When Croesus passes over the river Halys, he will overthrow the strength of an empire." Naturally, Croesus took this to mean that he would overthrow the enemy's empire ! But it was his own that he destroyed. Yet the oracle was right.

Pyrrhus, about to make war against Rome consulted the oracle, and received this answer. " Pyrrhus, you the Romans can conquer." This also reads either way ; he would conquer or be conquered. Yet another prince also received a double answer from the oracle. " You shall go shall return never you shall perish by the war." It is easily seen that the meaning altered according to the position of the stops.

Philip of Macedon, about to set forth to conquer Persia, also consulted the Delphic oracle and received the reply :

> " The ready victim crowned for death
> Before the altar stands."

Again the consultant took it for granted that it was his opponent who would be killed. Even in the Bible, we are told that when King Ahab was about to wage war on the Syrians, he asked the prophet Micaiah if Ramoth-Gilead would fall into his hands. The answer was, " Go, for the Lord will deliver the city into the hands of the king." But he did not say which king !

Besides this Delphic oracle, other famous ones were those of Jupiter at Dodona and Ammon, Delos, and of Venus in Paphos.

The Greek philosophers also gave much attention to the subject of dreams, though their opinion concerning their cause and their meanings differed.

Plato attached a physical cause to dreams, attributing them to disorders of the liver, which was then held to be the seat of the passions as well as of appetite. Cicero, too, attributed dreams to material and bodily causes, while even such learned psychologists as Democritus and Aristotle considered that dreams were the mental effects of bodily strain caused by the work during the day. The physician Galen, held that dreams were a warning of bodily health ; but the main bulk of the people believed firmly in dreams as mediums of communication between the gods and humanity, and they consulted the diviner or interpreter of dreams as moderns consult their doctor, paying him to unravel the problems set them in their sleep. Amongst the poorer classes, the dream events were considered as real as their day experiences, for they believed that the dreamer's soul was set free and visited its friends, whether living or dead ; they believed too that the souls of the living and the dead were able to communicate with the dreamer, and there is no doubt that as civilisation proceeded and more proofs were recorded, dreams were held to be of divine origin.

We have the Biblical examples, which we shall give

further on, of the dreams of Pharaoh, interpreted by Joseph, of whom it was said amongst his own people, " Lo, the Dreamer cometh." Then there are the dreams of King Abimelech, warned against taking Abraham's wife (whom the patriarch had falsely called his sister) ; also the dreams of Jacob and Laban, and those of Solomon and of Daniel. Later, come the visions of Joan of Arc, while John Bunyan was called the " Mad Dreamer " after he had written his immortal *Pilgrim's Progress.* Nearer still to modern times, we have Coleridge, who claimed to have written his poem, " Kubla Khan," from a dream.

Even amongst the American Indians, dreams played a prominent part, especially amongst those famous tribes the Hurons and the Iroquois, the latter inaugurating the New Year, which varied from the months of January to March, with a series of ceremonies, a "festival of Dreams," held also by the Hurons. These lasted several days and even weeks, and was a time of general freedom to commit whatever deeds they liked.

There is no doubt, therefore, of the importance of dreams in the history of the world, and that many dreams have been " events " casting their shadow before. Numberless instances have been given in books and proved on the most credible authority. Some dreams or visions may be caused, or have resulted from prolonged prayer or meditation. The sub-conscious mind is impressed, and then later, released in sleep. A detailed vivid vision, follows, and appears to the dreamer with graphic effect, so that the question must necessarily arise as to whether dreams are a warning of actual happenings about to take place. There is every proof that many people have found their problems solved by dreams, when possibly the brain may have been clearer and more able to concentrate on the single aim and problem involved.

Numerous instances have been given of warnings, told in dreams. Some of these have been described as dealing with places and persons never seen previously by the dreamer, yet which were recognised afterwards as having been correct in the dream. In some cases, the " message dreams " may be explained scientifically, by telepathy, or thought-transference. In many cases the one who sends the thought message, does not know that he or she has sent it. The need is urgent, the mind of the sender is in very great distress, and the message goes forth to the person it is meant for, unconsciously. The one who receives it is in the best condition to get it, the body being passive—in sleep—as at such times the mind is more than usually receptive of impressions of this nature. Under the influence of such dreams or " messages," the dreamer will often awake and proceed to carry out the message thus given. In some cases a problem may be solved for the dreamer, the solution coming in dream form as a message.

Of dreams in which a knowledge of the future is shown, explanations differ. It has been clearly proved that the inner mind possesses extraordinary powers. It is un-hampered by the limitations of time or space. Australia is as near in thought as the picture hanging on the wall close by. Next month, next year, or even later, is but the exten-sion of the present time, seen as the present. In dreams, therefore, the inner mind exercises these great powers of clairvoyance and clairaudience—it sees and hears the future as if it were the present ; it sees and hears what is happening in the distance of time, as though it were happening in the present. The mind is dreaming, is believed to have a " mind body," which it is enabled to use outside the limits of time and space and roam freely through both ; for which reason, the future is apparently foretold in dreams. This may help also to solve a difficulty which may arise in the future. Often we dream that we see people and places which we are only destined to see at some future time. Other times we find when we see a place apparently for the' first time in our waking lives, that it seems so familiar, we feel we must have visited it before. In such a case, we may have seen it in a dream, though we have forgotten all about it till we see it in reality. That dream may have been given us for a purpose, to warn, or to help, according to circum-stances. The old Scripture passage which says " He giveth His Beloved sleep," when literally translated, reads, " He giveth to His Beloved *in* sleep," which has a very different meaning.

When dreams are concerned with action, the dreamer is either hurrying to arrive at a place, or struggling to

escape from one, or else eluding or finding a certain person.
In these cases, the sub-conscious mind may be living over
again distorted or elaborated incidents and impressions
which have been received in the daily waking life.   Care
must be taken therefore to distinguish between such dreams.
When dreams can be thus traced to daily occurrences, their
meaning is obviously due to physical and not spiritual causes.

Back in the dim past, in the early stages of the world's
history, wise men studied this subject, and the results of
their researches and experiences were handed down from one
generation to another.   Certain dreams were found to be
followed by certain events ; the dream of a particular
object was found to be followed by particular experiences,
and thus the meaning of dreams gradually became fixed and
were recorded.   Many of these interpretations have been
handed down from the time of the Assyrians and the Greeks,
who became noted for their great knowledge of the subject.

Countless books, too, have been written in modern times.
One great scientific work dealing with psychology, called
Fact and Fable in Psychology, written by Professor Jastrow,
and published some years ago, devoted considerable space
to the growth of analogy between dreams and their reputed
meaning.

In this book he gave many current beliefs which have
arisen, probably, by the correspondence in similarity between
the dream and its reputed meaning.   Some of these meanings
are obviously logical ; as for instance, to dream of ascending
a ladder predicted coming good fortune, of descending one,
the approach of poverty, or misfortune.   To dream of dirt or
mud, foretells that you will be abused, or become the subject
of slander.   To dream of being on stilts indicates that the
dreamer is puffed up with pride of his or her own abilities.
To dream of gathering fruit from an old tree foreshadows an
approaching legacy from an old person.   A dream of a clock
means death, if the hands stop, but if they continue to move,
a sick person will recover.   A dream of music means good
feeling between loved ones.

Every day objects entered very much into these old
dreams.   To dream of earthworms meant that there were
secret enemies, striving to ruin the dreamer.   A dream of
onions or garlic, meant the betrayal of secrets.   The loss of

a tooth, showed the loss of a friend. The loss of a rib, the death of husband or wife; the loss of a foot, a postponed journey. To dream of wading or swimming is good so long as the head be kept above water. If the dreamer falls or sinks, then trouble is approaching.

The saying that " Dreams go by contraries " has arisen from the fact that many dreams have been found to depend upon contrast, instead of similarity, for their interpretation. For instance, to dream of death has been proved to be followed by happiness and long life. The dream of a fall has been followed by a rise in life; or conversely, a sudden rise betokened a fall.

In some countries, too, the significance of a dream has altered according to the sex of the dreamer. The Maoris in New Zealand, and the African Zulus believe almost solely in contrary dreams. If a friend dies, then the dreamer will hear of his recovery. To dream of a wedding is to receive news of a death.

Some Wonderful Examples

As we have seen, the ancients believed in all good faith and reverence in dreams. The Scriptures say, " God speaketh once, yea twice, yet man perceiveth it not. In a dream, in a vision of the night, when deep sleep falleth upon men, in slumbering upon the bed, then he openeth the ears of men and sealeth their instruction."

Thus they looked upon dreams as direct messages from God, and regarded angels as His chosen messengers. When Jacob dreamed he beheld " a ladder, set upon earth, and the top of it reached to Heaven, and behold, the angels of God ascending and descending upon it." In his vision, " The Lord stood above it and said, I am the Lord God of Abraham, thy father, and the God of Isaac; the land whereon thou liest, to thee will I give it, and to thy seed."

Again in the old Testament, one reads " Hear now my words; If there be a prophet among you, I the Lord will make myself known to him in a vision and will speak to him in a dream." These words were spoken to Moses.

In these olden times, kings were not above seeking the services of soothsayers and dream interpreters. One of the best known examples is that of Pharaoh, when he dreamt

of the seven lean kine and the seven fat kine. When he
was troubled as to how to read this riddle, his chief butler,
who had already had his own dreams interpreted by Joseph,
told him about the young Israelite prisoner. Pharaoh at
once seized the opportunity, and Joseph versed in divining,
read the seven kine to be the coming fat years and lean years,
of plenty and famine.

Another Biblical ruler, Nebuchadnezzar dreamt that he
saw a great image of gold, silver, brass, iron and clay.
But when he awoke, he could not remember the details of
the dream. Accordingly he summoned the sorcerers and
known interpreters, even sending for men of the Chaldeans,
a race especially noted for their gifts in interpreting dreams.
He ordered them not only to interpret the dream itself
but to tell him the full details which he himself had forgotten.
Here surely was a problem indeed, and it is not surprising
that one and all failed to produce an answer to these unreasonable demands. Equally, in those days of complete
despotism, it is not surprising that one and all were
condemned to be put to death, amongst them Daniel, who
" had understanding in all dreams and visions," and he
appealed to the Captain of the king's guard to stay his
hand and allow him to try.

Then Daniel, we are told, not only succeeded in actually
dreaming the dream himself, but convinced Nebuchadnezzar
of the probable meaning. He thereby saved the life of
himself and his fellow interpreters. The dream itself is
interesting, as it is one that might well be considered as an
adventure into the future. The king had dreamt that
this image was made of various substances ; " his head was
of fine gold, his breast and his arms of silver, his body and
thighs of brass, his feet and legs part iron, part clay. Then
a stone smote the image upon its feet that were of iron and
clay, and brake them into pieces. Then was the iron, the
clay, the brass, the silver and the gold broken in pieces and
became like the chaff of the threshing floor."

Then Daniel interpreted the dream. The image was
the welded kingdoms, over which Nebuchadnezzar ruled.
He, according to the wisdom of Daniel, was the golden
" head," the other kingdoms beneath him were to be broken
up by wars, and only the one kingdom, that of Nebuchad-

nezzar, should remain triumphant to the end. This interpretation was not only pleasing to the king, but fulfilled the interpretation in every way, and made it an additional proof of the veracity of dreams.

We have, too, the dreams of Jacob and Elijah.

In the New Testament, St. Paul dreamed that " The Lord stood by him and said, ' Be of good cheer, Paul, for as thou hast testified of me in Jerusalem, so must thou also at Rome'." Later, Paul's dream message was " Fear not, Paul, thou must be brought before Cæsar, and Lo, God has given thee all them that sail with thee."

This dream differs from those of Pharaoh and of Nebuchadnezzar, inasmuch as it is a direct message, while the others were symbolic parables needing the interpretation of a gifted diviner.

Throughout the ages, famous writers have devoted books to dreams. Homer tells how his heroes were helped by dreams sent by Zeus through his messenger Hermes (in Latin, Mercury). One story relates how Perseus is sent to kill the Gorgon, of the " snaky locks," and on whom to gaze, meant instant death. In a dream, Perseus beholds the goddess of wisdom, Pallas Athene (Minerva). She bids him polish his shield so that he shall see the reflection of the Gorgon and kill her without looking directly on her face.

Artemidorus, another famous Greek historian of the second century A.D., believed that dreams differed in their meanings according to the personality of the dreamer, and he wrote many books on the subject, recording prophetic dreams that had come true.

One of these was concerning a dream of Alexander the Great. In this dream Alexander saw a Satyros (Satyr) dancing on his shield. At the time the city of Tyros was in a state of siege, and Alexander sent for his own diviner, Aristander, to interpret the dream. Aristander did so by making a play on words. He divided Satyros into two words, meaning " Thine (is) Tyros." It encouraged Alexander to renew the attack on the city, and he speedily forced it to yield.

Coming to later times we find many famous interpreters, including the wizard Merlin, at the Court of King Arthur, and in the seventh century, the Venerable Bede, monk and historian.

Probably one of the most famous dreamers of all in the middle ages was Joan of Arc, who dreamed that she was destined to save France. But it is not perhaps so widely known that a generation before her day, another girl, Marie d'Avignon, dreamed of arms and armour. In her dream she thrust them away, saying she was but a woman and had no use for such war-like implements. Then she was told that they were intended for a maid who would come forward and rescue France from the invader. Later, when Joan's own visions of her saints and angels were known widely enough to bring her to the notice of the Dauphin, this other dream, too, was remembered. Bernard Shaw in his play, puts into her mouth, the very apt and probable answer which she might well have given in reality, when charged with the accusation that her dream voices " come from your imagination." " Of course " she replies, " that is how the messages of God do come to us."

" Nobody," writes the author in his preface, " disputes that the relief of Orleans, followed by the Coronation of the Dauphin at Rheims, saved France. Yet Joan was a young peasant maid, unlearned and unversed in either war or politics. How did her great and successful schemes enter her mind unless when in the dream state, some other great mind had been able to influence hers and use her brain as a messenger.

Socrates, Luther, Swedenborg, all saw visions and had dreams, and so through the different ages to modern times, instances constantly occur which are too important to ignore, and too accurate to dismiss as idle fancies.

A modern author states that he dreamed vividly of a visit to a seaside resort, which he had never seen before. In his dream he saw himself driving down the main street from the railway station to an hotel on the front, where he watched the tide come in for some little time before turning down a side street to a café *where he knew* they made excellent coffee. The dream was so impressed upon his mind that he took the first opportunity of visiting the town in question, went straight to the hotel he had seen in his dream and then turned down the side street where he found the identical café he had dreamed of entering. This type of dream is by no means uncommon, but it is very

difficult to explain, as it is obviously not a warning or premonition either of good or evil—it is merely a peculiar experience
which raises the question as to whether in very deep sleep,
the spirit or mentality can ignore physical space.

Another curious experience for which the writer can
vouch, is that of falling asleep at a writing table, pen in
hand, and finding on awaking, a sheet of paper which
had been blank before sleeping, now covered with curious
Eastern-looking characters which the dreamer was unable
to decipher, until taking them to a student of Arabic, he
learned that they were written in that language, of which
the writer, in a waking state, knew nothing.

Much of our knowledge concerning dreams comes to us
from the East, and from sources that are many centuries old,
but it would not be accurate for the Western world to accept
all these, as certain articles would not have the same associa-
tion amongst people of such widely differing mentality and
mode of living. For instance, the peacock, in the East,
was considered a sacred bird, and it meant death for anyone
except a priest, to possess even a single feather—hence,
perhaps, the popular belief that peacock's feathers are
unlucky. This idea still lingers, for even in the Western
world, few people will give peacocks feathers house-room, or
not feel that even a dream of them presages evil.

Other wonderful examples of dreams were given some
years ago in a book called *The Other World*, written by
the Reverend F. G. Lee. One or two of these dreams are
worthy of reference, as they are vouched for and given in
the very words of the dreamer.

A gentleman in Cornwall dreamed that he witnessed a
murder of the Chancellor of the Exchequer, in the House of
Commons. He himself had never seen the place or even a
picture of it, but he told several people of this dream and
described the dress, and the position in the lobby of the
murderer and his victim. Next day—this happened a
hundred years ago—a rider with the news came to the village,
and he confirmed the circumstances of the tragedy. Soon
afterwards the gentleman himself went to London, and was
taken to the House of Commons where, in the lobby of the
House, he pointed out where he had seen in his dream, the
chancellor and his assailant stand. Those who had been

present at the time of the tragedy, testified to the fact that the murder had taken place on that spot, just as the dreamer had described.

Another striking and famous example was that which occurred to the mother of Maria Marten. Her daughter had left home with a man named Frederick Corder. Under promise of marriage, he betrayed her, and later murdered her. Time passed, and the supposed husband of Maria wrote to the mother to say that they were now married and were living happily abroad. But Mrs. Marten was not satisfied ; she dreamed that her daughter was dead and had been buried in a barn. So strong was her impression of this dream that eventually she caused a search to be made. The body of Maria was discovered and bore signs of foul play. Corder was arrested and made to stand his trial. He was found guilty and condemned to death, and he confessed his crime. He was executed in 1828. But the story became so famous that it has been made into both book and play. It was known as " Maria Marten, or The Murder at the Red Barn."

One outstanding feature of dreams is the frequency of incidents of falling and of flying, even far back in the early history of the world. The latter is due probably to the Greek belief in Hermes or Mercury as the flying messenger and god of dreams. Cicero refers to dreams of flying. St. Jerome mentions in his Memoirs his dreams of flight, and Cervantes in his famous book, *Don Quixote*, tells of falling ; how " It has happened many times to me," says the innkeeper's daughter, " to dream that I was falling down from a tower and never coming to the ground, and when I awoke from the dream to find myself as weak and shaken as if I had really fallen."

This falling dream happens, however, to most of us, and some people will tell you that it is a memory of our very early monkey ancestors who often fell from the branches of trees. Few people, however, will accept this explanation ; a far more likely interpretation is the recurrence of a memory of a fall and which may really have happened months ago.

But flying in dreams has occurred to many famous people, long before the rise of real aviation.

Raffaelli, the eminent French painter, confessed that so

vividly had he dreamed of floating in the air, that on awaking, he arose and tried to repeat his adventure, but naturally, failed.

Herbert Spencer, the writer, in his book *Principles of Sociology*, mentions that when in company with a dozen people, no less than three testified that they had dreamed so vividly of flying, that they had actually made attempts when awake, one of them having injured his leg.

The most famous writer on Dreams, Professor Freud, held that the dream of flying was the bridge to the concealed wish to fly, and the mind set free in sleep, proceeded to carry out the secret wish of the dreamer, performing with the astral body, what was not possible for the material one to do.

Many famous works and acts have been done, or resulted from dreams. Of books one might say again "there is no end." One of the earliest writers on dreams is Dr. Simon Forman, an astrologer who lived in the year 1600. In his *Autobiography*, he says, that as a child of six, directly he fell asleep, he saw visions of mighty mountains rolling down on him, yet from which he always escaped and got to the top. Then he would see many great waters like to drown him, yet he thought he did overpass them." And these dreams and visions which he had every night for several years, he believed were sent him by God to signify the troubles of his later years, and which he was thus encouraged that he would overcome.

De Quincy in his famous book, *Confessions of an English Opium Eater*, described his adventures from dreams.

In music, we find the great composer Richard Wagner writing in his diary, when he was in love with Mathilde Wesendonk, after a dream, "As I awoke I distinctly felt your kiss on my brow."

More detailed is the story of Tartini and his famous work, *Trille de Diable*. He tells how one night when working at a composition, he could not get it to his satisfaction, and at last went to bed. He awoke, as he thought, to find the devil seated on his bed post. To him, Tartini handed his violin, and the devil played the now famous Trill. When he awoke, Tartini realised that it was a dream, but wrote down what he could remember of the music, and it has been played by every great violinist since.

Books galore have been written on dreams and re-appearances, and Du Maurier's most famous book, *Peter Ibbetson*, records serial dreams of union with a beloved woman after her death, said to be based on real experiences.

Another remarkable instance was that of a rector of a certain parish, one of whose congregation had recently died. The deceased was a rich man, but believed to have left no will. Great injustice would have been caused by this, as the estates would then pass to a distant branch of the family, leaving those who had really a right to it, in dire straits. The rector dreamed the dead man appeared to him, and told him that a will had been made. Not only one dream, but three came to the rector, and each time fresh details were given. On the last occasion the rector dreamed that he himself went to London, to Staple Inn (a place to which he had never been). He was directed to a certain house and to a particular room. He was told that a picture of Lord Eldon hung in the room, and also other details, such as a particular drawer in which the missing will had been placed.

So vivid was the dream that the rector told it to a clerical friend, who accompanied him to London. They went to Staple Inn, and in the office, they found the room, the drawer, and the will.

Here is a clear case of a dead person aware of the pain his acts or omission of act had caused, who had done his best to get it amended, using the mind of the rector, perhaps a more sensitive man than most, as a form of medium or a mental receiving set. It seems to point to the fact of the survival of the spirit, as well as the activity of the sub-conscious mind of the receiver of the message.

But messages can also come from the living. A sailor in the Channel Islands dreamed very vividly of people in great danger, and who were calling him from some rocks. He awoke, but directly he fell asleep, the dream returned to him. Very early in the morning, he went down to the pier and told his comrades. They were inclined to laugh at him at first, but as he persisted in his assertions, they at last launched a boat, and set forth to a rocky islet. To their amaze, they found some shipwrecked people, nearly dead with hunger, cold and exposure. Their boat had capsized, and they had united in praying for help and wishing for the boatman, from whom probably they had taken the boat, to come to their help. A lighthouse was built afterwards on this spot.

The writer is aware of another " message " dream. Two brothers lived near to one another, both alone in their respective houses. One was taken ill in the night but had no means of communicating with the other. Yet desperate, he willed with all his strength of mind and will power to have his brother with him. Mechanically he noted the time, and at last fell asleep. Very early the brother came to him, letting himself in with the duplicate key, and he sent for doctor and nurses. Afterwards he asked if his brother knew the time when he had been taken ill. The other said, " it was just half-past three."

Then the other brother said : " I woke at that hour. I had just dreamt that our father (who had recently died) was standing by me, evidently troubled. It seemed silly to get up at that hour and come here, so I forced myself to go to sleep again." Clearly here was another instance of a telepathic and bodily message conveyed through the medium of the dead.

There are countless other instances, and there are probably few people who cannot relate some strange dream occurrence, proving that dreams are valuable, and not to be scoffed at or taken lightly. Some of the most famous men in the world have not been ashamed to take credence of their dreams.

Napoleon believed in his dreams, and probably had he followed their warnings, the retreat from Moscow might not have taken place.

Bismarck, the great German minister, also believed in dreams and had his own dreams interpreted many times before proceeding on any momentous course of action.

In religious circles, too, dreams have not been treated lightly.

Pope Innocent IV, when lying ill, was warned of his approaching death. He fell asleep and dreamt that he saw a favourite cleric, Robert Grosthead, the Bishop of Lincoln, enter his room. Approaching the Pope's bedside, and pointing to him, the Bishop said, " Arise, and come to Judgment."

When the Pope awakened, the dream remained in his memory, and despite the physicians around him, he made all preparations for his death, which took place a few days later.

Another famous dream was related by Professor Freud, of Delboeuf, a great French philosopher. He (Delboeuf) dreamt that the courtyard of his house was covered with snow, buried in which he found two little lizards. Picking them up he warmed them and put them into a crevice of the wall, and gave them some fern leaves, which he called by its right name *Asplenium ruta muralis*. In his waking state Delboeuf knew nothing of this plant, and on waking, he could not understand how he had known the name of it. It was not till many years later that Delboeuf found that he had seen a collection of ferns, with their names, and the occurrence had been completely forgotten till in sleep the memory came back to him.

In early history, too, people thought that sailors and soldiers had special significance in their dreams. For instance, if a sailor dreamed his ship was going into battle, and getting beaten, then he was advised to take special care of his conduct and actions during the ensuing week, lest harm befall him. Conversely, if his ship was winning the fight, then good would follow. The sailor who dreamt that his ship had been wrecked was warned to look well after his personal belongings lest they be stolen by an envious ship-mate.

If a married sailor while abroad dreamt of his wife or sweetheart, it indicated approaching trouble and that his help might be needed. To dream of his children meant that he might soon be expected to be invalided home to them speedily.

In some cases these dreams went by contraries, as for instance, if a sailor's wife or sweetheart dreamt that her husband or sweetheart was in trouble, then he was probably sailing in calm waters.

The worst omen was the one that showed the sailor husband or sweetheart wearing a medal. Then bad news of wounds or even death might follow.

The soldiers' dreams, too, were of importance. If he dreamt that he was in battle, it foreshadowed early promotion. A dream of punishment denoted the coming of a quarrel between comrades. Good fortune would come from a dream of being wounded in battle, also to dream of his folk at home, while on active service, but if he dreamt that the war were over and he was back in his home, then he was warned to take care of himself and avoid undue risks.

The soldier's wife also was not forgotten, for although she might dream that her man was killed in battle, yet it might only mean a wound. The worst military omen was to see her husband or sweetheart decorated with medals, for this betokened future poverty.

SECTION II

SCIENTIFIC EXPLANATIONS OF THE DREAMING STATE

IT is agreed by modern scientists that there is good ground for believing that in the dream state, the mind, soul or consciousness—whichever we may prefer to call it—is enabled to do things which are not possible to it in the ordinary waking state.

In sleep, some of the faculties of the mind are still working, though they may give back to the waking state very few impressions of what has happened to them. Sleep allows free play to the sub-conscious mind of the individual. His mental powers are quickened in sleep, in contrast to the body which is resting inert. It is often found that a problem which has presented many difficulties during the day seems to be solved after the person " has slept on it." In the morning some fresh angle or solution appears. There may not be any knowledge of what has happened in many cases, but the probability is that the sub-conscious mind at work during the night has solved the unknown factors which had lain hidden. In hypnotism, which is only a deep sleep, its very name derived from Hypnos (the Greek God of Sleep), though produced by artificial means, the strong will working on a weaker one, the mind works very clearly, and shows that once " asleep " beneath the will of the hypnotiser, it possesses powers to make discoveries and to act out of all ordinary run of things.

The scientific explanation of this state is, that the mind may be considered as consisting of two parts—the ordinary or objective mind, and the inner or subjective mind.

It is the inner mind that works principally while the body sleeps, either in ordinary or hypnotic state, and which also helps the individual in moments of grave danger, as manifested by what we term instinctive action.

When the body is dulled by sleep or unconsciousness, the inner mind has a chance to escape, as it were, from its attention to the affairs of the body. It is released from its chains and can work more easily upon outside matters. This explains why in moments of danger, or when death is near, although the body is incapable of movement, the mind is able to project itself and make an impression on persons at a distance. It may then appear as an apparition which tries to give a message to some loved one. It may be thought that this has little to do with actual dreams, but really it is most important, for if we can establish the fact that the mind can act almost independently of the body during sleep, we shall be able to see that some dreams are real, and may well be taken as solemn warnings or visions as to what is to happen in the future.

This brings us perhaps into conflict with what we may call the natural order of time. All our waking experiences tend to show us that all things happen in a certain order; past, present and the future. All that happens daily is the direct outcome of the past, of something that has already happened. The present, therefore, is the " child of the past." The future is just as inevitably the child of the present. Now if the future is really caused by the present, then there is no reason why we should not foresee it. This makes prophecies possible, and dreams may be the form in which the future is foretold. Time is but a convenient ·expression made by man. In reality, there is no such thing as Time ; there is neither past, present, nor future. Everything must be considered as a part of the Universe ; as an Eternal Now. The links that bind the past, present and future into one whole, are such that there can be no separation into such parts. To the limited mind of man, to whom things are presented by means of his bodily eyes, these things as happen seem to be so divided. But to the inner mind there is no such thing as Time or Space. It is just one plane, a part of the great Eternal Mind, or Universe, to which there can be neither past, present nor future ; no beginning or end. The links of the chain are but dimly seen, and a glimpse of what is to come is obtained only at times by this inner mind of ours. Some people are more sensitive in mind than others, and to these will come back the dream actions and memories of the inner mind.

Even the ancients believed this. Tertullian, who lived two hundred years before the birth of Christ, believed that dreams were the spiritual life of the soul. Hippocrates, another famous doctor and philosopher, believed too that when the dreams were not caused by bodily ill-health, the spirit left the body when asleep, and roamed to and fro, actions performed afterwards being due to the knowledge that the soul or spirit had gained in its wanderings.

Many people believe not only in dreams while the body is asleep at night, but in dreams that may be held during the day. By intense concentration on their ideas, the body may be left behind, while the brain or mind works out its conceptions.

The musician, the painter, the novelist, the architect, the sculptor, and the poet, have their dreams and visions in their ordinary waking state, and all the beauty of their work is the outcome of it. In some cases the work is actually the result of a real dream. R. L. Stevenson's wonderful story of Dr. Jekyll and Mr. Hyde was a dream.

Artistic creation—for example, the work of the musician or painter—in the day-dream state is nearly always accomplished while the body is almost wholly at rest. The artist is not conscious of his bodily surroundings. He is living for the moment in a dream state—another world—the world of visions. He sees and hears things with the eyes and ears of the inner mind—with that finer sense which is given to the ordinary person only in sleep, and then not too often.

Many of our dreams we cannot recall. We wake in the morning knowing that we have dreamed beautiful things, or sorrowful things, but we cannot remember the details of them. This means that we have not yet learned to bring them back to our waking state to be made of use to us.

But yet they may actually be present to the inner mind as warnings which are acted upon without our consciously knowing them. We make decisions to do this, or not to do that, without quite knowing why we do so. But really we have been guided by a dream.

In an earlier part of this section it was suggested that the power of dreaming and seeing visions was to be attributed to the inner or subjective unconscious mind transcending the limitations of time and space. There are, however, other explanations which are worth attention.

Inherited Memories

Racial or inherited memory, or the stored-up impressions in the mind, which are assumed to be transmitted down through the ages for countless generations, are said to account for many dreams. When we sleep we are less able to control ourselves than at any other time. It is then that the remembrances of a long-vanished past surge over us.

Perhaps stored in a single brain-cell lies the concentrated impression of an exciting incident in the life of some far-off ancestor. A chance thought may cause the cell to stir, as it were, in the sub-conscious brain while the body sleeps, and the result is a vivid and lengthy dream complete and accurate in detail, apparently unaccountable, as it usually deals with life in some bygone century, or even a past civilisation long dead, but in truth a memory of a past reality, embroidered by the sub-conscious mind of a modern brain in much the same way as an ancient legend is skilfully retold and embroidered by the mind of a modern novelist.

These dreams are not so much warnings of what is to happen as reconstructions of what has happened. We live again fragments of the lives of our ancestors in the dim past. We think and act as they did, see the things they saw. We love, fear and hate, as they did.

Often when we wake we are only barely conscious of the strangeness of these dreams. We have lost the sequence, the continuity of the thoughts and sights and actions. We just know that we have lived through weird and distressing or brave and gallant adventures. It is by the great differences we have felt that we have been made aware of the gap between those times and our own. Frequently, such dreams as these are given as evidence of the re-incarnation of the spirit from one life to another, but it would seem that this opinion is a case of " the wish is father to the thought," and the material or scientific explanation of the remembrance is in favour of the transmission of brain-cells rather than re-incarnation of souls, poetic as the theory may be.

Spiritual Influences

Another explanation of these vivid dreams held, is that they are due to the influence of departed spirits. At death, it is suggested, only the material part of the body dies, the soul or spirit survives, and it is this surviving individuality that needs perhaps to convey some warning, or make some other communication to members of the ordinary world. Such a spirit takes the opportunity of finding a mind suitably free in sleep, upon which it endeavours to impress its message.

The dreamer is unconscious of this external influence, and feels and acts in his dream-state as though he were actually living through this experience himself. If the dream is a vivid one, it will persist in his mind and have some effect in modifying his actions in his waking life.

Inspiration is thought to be of this type of dream. In our dream life we are helped by these discarnate intelligences in this way. On other occasions it may be that people are tempted and counselled wrongly by the same causes. The souls who have passed over are not all those of good people. Many of them are the spirits of wrong-doers, still eager for the chance of making their influence for evil effective. Deprived of a physical vehicle for work on the earth plane, they wait till an opportunity is afforded of using another body as the channel for their own evil-doing. In sleep one may lay aside not only the body but a part of one's mental armour as well. The enemy is then able to get through the defences as it were and influence the mind for bad. For this reason, before committing the body to sleep, the spiritual armour of prayer should be brought into action. An invocation to the Greatest Power of all will give the sleeper fresh powers of resistance to evil, so that he or she may sleep in confidence, knowing that protection will be afforded.

The Theory of Re-incarnation

There is just one more quoted explanation of dreams, and that is of re-incarnation, perhaps the most picturesque of all, but one that is invariably rejected by scientists. The idea that in sleep we return to past lives and live over again many adventures and incidents, is but an unproven theory, and with which most people must agree, since all the evidence that can be taken to confirm this idea can usually be explained by the more natural and therefore more probable theory of inheritance, by racial and ancestral resemblance, transmitted by the brain cells or even history, from one generation to another.

However, " we *know* we dream, we *dream* we know," is the only answer to those who " lay down the law " as to the mystery of dreams.

The theory of re-incarnation, however, pre-supposes that the human soul in each body has lived countless lives before the present one. Between each life and the next there may be a long rest, perhaps for centuries, and the body we use at the present time knows nothing of the previous existence of the soul which now inhabits it.

One could not expect the suit of clothes worn last year and destroyed, to know or show signs of anything happening this year to a fresh suit. But the man who wore both, would know what happened to each. So with man, it is the soul, the wearer of the earthly body which persists, and it is the soul alone that knows.

In sleep, the soul is set free from the hampering body and its limitations ; it then knows what happened to it in its previous lives ; can live these over again in recollection.

It has glimpses here and there of its past experiences. Some of these are dimly remembered and brought back to the waking consciousness. In other cases the soul, knowing its own immortality, is able to glean and bring back some ideas of its immediate future. It *knows* what is to happen, and tries to warn and guide its material body aright—to direct it amid the stream of impressions it is receiving minute by minute, which distract it and lead it astray.

At present all scientific investigation of the matter by modern methods is only in its infancy, and that which is still a mystery at the moment may some day be established as above doubt and subject to laws as natural as those of Radio !

The Analogy of Wireless

If some advanced thinker of early days had been able to establish a wireless transmitter and receiver, for instance, between a beseiged castle in the middle ages and the tents of the beseiging enemy encamped outside, he would have been accused of dealings with the Evil One and he and his wireless set destroyed straightway in terror. Yet had such an instrument been in existence at the time, pages of mediaeval history would have been altered. The point of this argument as it affects the usefulness of dreams is that the laws of wireless and the forces which made it possible were *there all the time*, only man, in his mental ignorance and scientific undevelopment, was unable to use it.

Dreams, and the sub-conscious powers in ourselves and others which manifest themselves as dreams, may be a kind of spiritual wireless obeying natural spiritual laws, if we only were able to learn their nature and apply them at will, which is exactly what modern science is attempting to do.

The tested meanings of centuries may be the ground-work on which great discoveries are to be made at some future time, and until then we can only take these meanings as a starting point and test them for ourselves as our own dreams occur. It is a fascinating study and one of which we are as yet only on the " fringes of exploration."

One theory, however, modern investigation has established beyond doubt, and that is the theory of the sub-conscious mind as an explanation of nine dreams out of ten. This fact, however, does not in any way detract from the fascination of the subject, nor does it account for the " tenth dream," which we may explain as our individual tastes prefer. But it does explain and clarify those little puzzling, confused dreams which make us almost ashamed to remember or recount them ; and this is in itself a good thing, as it raises the subject to one of respectful treatment by the medical profession, thus paving the way for the " tenth dream " to be treated seriously as a possible means of spiritual communication.

The theory of the sub-conscious mind is a scientific elaboration of the line written by Defoe as early as 1726 : " To dream is nothing else but to sleep thinking." Nine dreams out of ten, then, are a mental mirror for our daily thoughts, which accounts for these curious features of dreams.

(1) That our dreams are mostly a series of pictures, which we sometimes *see* ourselves taking part.

(2) That these pictures are frequently distorted reflections of subjects that have recently occupied our minds.

(3) That, as in mirrors, we sometimes see our thoughts reversed, which accounts perhaps for the many dreams whose meanings are said to " go by contraries."

When, therefore, our dreams are as grotesque and unnatural as the reflections in the distorting mirrors to be found at fairs and other places of amusement, then we must lay the blame, not on the faculty of dreaming, but on the quality and condition of the mental mirror. Physical conditions and the kind of thoughts entertained habitually and especially just before going to sleep, will adjust the condition of the mental mirror to the desired state.

The benefit of the theory of sub-conscious thought in dreams, is that it will frequently lead a person who is disturbed in either mind or in health to the exact cause of the disturbance, and ultimately to its cure, by correct reading and noting of constantly occurring dreams. For instance, should the cause of mental disturbance be a problem either personal, or perhaps the mislaying of an important article, during healthy sleep—never during drugged sleep—the sub-conscious mind, freed from the burden of daily thoughts and actions, will follow natural logical processes, bringing to the surface—and thus reflecting on the mental mirror—one detail after another which will assist in the deduction of the answer, till finally the solution of the problem is thrown upon the mirror in one complete picture, and the dreamer awakes quite confident of the whereabouts of the article, or the answer to his personal problem, often without being aware of as to how he obtained this knowledge, which in reality, his dreams have enabled him to dig up *out of his own mind.* No one should be ashamed therefore to look up apparently trifling, or even what may appear to be foolish dreams, as they may be when gathered together and correctly read, the means of helping the dreamer to solve the difficulties of his own daily life ; in fact, they may help us to help ourselves, which is after all, the greatest aid Fate can give us.

That this idea is exploited also is proved by people who follow a sleep-walker. Here, however, it is not so much the matter of a dream, as it is the brain, following out orders in duplication. That is to say, the body has committed certain acts during the day, and at night, the brain still impressed with the commands given it, causes the body to re-enact the actions by letting its owner " walk in his sleep."

In the next section of this book, we give a selection of dream interpretations, many of which have been handed down to us from early Roman times, and are given together with the more modern meanings. Some of these old interpretations are the work of one, Artemidorus, who lived in the reign of Antoninus and wrote a book of dreams, which was later translated by Rigaltius. An edition of this book was later published in 1604.

SECTION III

DREAMS AND THEIR MEANINGS

Ancient and Modern Interpretations

N.B.—Ancient meanings marked (Anc.). Modern meanings, where Ancient meaning also given, are marked (Mod.).

A

Abandon.—This is an unfavourable dream, and indicates the loss of friends, or the failure of some fortunate expectation.

Abyss.—To dream of any hollow space is a sign of difficulties ahead. Be careful in your business affairs.

Accident.—If the accident occurs at sea, it means disappointment in your love affairs ; but if it happens on land, it concerns your business ventures.

Acorn.—(to see) ill news or slander ; (to gather) a legacy.

Acquaintance.—To dream that you fight with them signifies distraction, especially if the person so dreaming be sick.

Adversary.—To dream that you receive obstructions from him, shows that you shall despatch your business speedily. (Anc.)

Aeroplane.—A sign of rising fortunes unless it should crash, which forebodes failure in business.

Age.—A health dream ; if you see yourself as very old, it indicates a coming illness, but to see other people old indicates recovery.

Air.—To dream that you see it clear and serene denotes the recovery of lost goods. If the person so dreaming be at law, it shows he shall overthrow his adversary, and if he designs a journey it shows he shall be successful therein. (Anc.)

Almonds.—To dream one sees or eats almonds signifies difficulty and trouble. (Anc.) Peace and successful enterprise. (Mod.)

Alms.—To dream they are begged of you, and you deny to give, forebodes want and misery to the dreamer, but should he give them freely denotes great joy to the dreamer. (Anc.)

34

Altar.—To dream that you see an Altar betokens joy and gladness. (Anc.)

Anchor.—Above water, and clearly seen, is a good sign ; but under water, betokens disappointment.

Angels.—This is an excellent dream, showing increase of honours and authority. (Anc.)

Anger.—A dream of contrary. If you are angry in your dream with someone you know, it shows that you will benefit in some way through that person, or if it is a stranger, some unexpected good news will reach you.

Angling.—A dream of contraries, if you make a catch it forebodes ill, but if you are unsuccessful it is a good sign. (Anc.)

Animals.—To see wild animals, or any unusual creature, is a bad omen. Domestic animals have separate meanings ; the cat and dog mean enemies, unless you kill them. Cows and bulls are a good sign, if peaceful, but denote business difficulties if they attack you.

Ants.—These indicate business prosperity, but in fresh surroundings.

Ape.—Enemies and deceit are indicated.

Apples.—To see apples, means good fortune ; to eat, disappointment.

Apple-tree.—Good news will soon reach you.

Army.—An obstacle dream foretelling difficulty, unless fighting, in which case it foretells serious trouble.

Artichoke.—Vexations and troubles, which, however, you will surmount.

Ashes.—Indicates misfortunes and losses.

Asparagus.—A sign of good fortune.

Asps.—A warning of danger which only your own bravery and forethought can avert.

Asylum.—To see the inside of an asylum forebodes serious trouble, but if you do not enter the building, it is merely a warning of difficulties to be overcome.

B

Baby.—It is a curious fact that it is fortunate to see children in a dream if they are old enough to be independent, but a helpless baby is a bad sign. It shows some disappointment in love or a serious illness in the family.

Bag.—A sign of better times, especially if a heavy one.

Bagpipes.—As with most unusual things, when seen in a dream, this musical instrument is not a favourable sign, and in particular it indicates matrimonial worry and difficulty. (Anc.)

Baker or Baking.—To see another person baking is a

good sign in every way ; you will not have to wait long for some favourable turn of events. But if you yourself are baking, it indicates the serious illness of someone dear to you.

Balcony.—This dream should be classed among the obstacle omens, though the difficulty to be faced will not be a serious one.

Bacon.—An unfortunate omen, whatever happens in the dream, whether you are eating it or merely buying it. Generally it concerns the health.

Balloon.—Another unusual omen, and therefore an un favourable sign for the dreamer.

Barber.—To dream that you are in a Barber's shop, fore-tells losses and difficulties in business.

Barley Bread.—To dream of eating it signifies health and content. (Anc.)

Basket.—An obstacle dream, since it is so easy to upset the contents. Be careful of your business ventures or you will lose money.

Bat.—Treachery is clearly shown when you dream about these curious nocturnal creatures. Beware of discussing your plans. Do not lend money and avoid all speculation.

Basin.—To dream you are eating or drinking from a basin is an unnatural dream ; if you are in love, you must expect difficulty, and may not marry the first object of your affections.

Bath and Bathing.—If it is in the open, and the water is clear, it shows success in business ; but if dirty, troubles and difficulties.

Beating.—If a married man dreams that he is beating his wife, it is a very fortunate sign and denotes married happiness and a comfortable home. But for lovers, it is considered a bad dream. It is also fortunate if a man dreams that he is beating some woman who is not his wife. In the same way, if a father or mother dreams that they are punishing one of their own children, it is a fortunate sign, but not if the child is a stranger.

Bed.—To dream that you are in a strange bed, shows some unexpected good turn in your business affairs ; if you are in your own bed, it concerns your love affairs. To dream of making a bed is a sign of a change of residence. To sit on a bed is a sign of an early marriage.

Beer.—To dream that you are drinking Beer or Ale, is a sign of some monetary loss in connection with speculation. If you only see the Ale or Beer, or if other people are drinking it, but not yourself, the loss will be small. For all that you should be careful in betting or speculating.

Bees.—This is a good omen, unless they sting you in your dream. They concern business matters, however, not love or friendship. (Anc.)

Bells.—To dream that one hears ringing of Bells, if of a sanguine complexion, brings good news ; but to others it shows alarms, disturbances and commotions among citizens. (Anc.)

Bicycle.—To dream that you are riding one means that you will have to make an important decision. Think well, and then act as you think best.

Bier.—If you are lying upon it, it signifies a happy ending to your hopes.

Billiards.—To play, indicates some difficulty ; if you are in love, or engaged, it means that you will be opposed by your betrothed's family.

Bills.—To dream that you are paying them denotes speedy financial gains ; that they are unpaid, signifies evil speaking.

Birds.—If you are poor and struggling, Birds indicate a coming improvement in your circumstances. But if you are wealthy, you may expect a reverse. It is a good sign if the Birds show beautiful plumage. If the Birds are singing, it is always fortunate.

Birth.—It is a good sign when a married woman dreams of giving birth to a child ; but for the single woman it foretells trouble in the near future.

Blindness.—To dream of Blind people or that you yourself lose your sight is the sign of an unfortunate love affair.

Blood.—To dream of Blood in any form is the sign of a severe disappointment. If you yourself are bleeding anywhere it indicates an unfortunate love affair or a quarrel with some valued friend.

Blows.—A dream of contrary meaning. If you receive Blows in your dream, it shows a reconciliation after a quarrel, or some good fortune coming to you from a friend. To give Blows to other people is, however, a sign of trouble.

Boat or Ship.—If you dream that you are sailing and that the water is smooth, it indicates some fortunate business or happiness in married life. If the water is rough, then you will have to face many difficulties. If you fall into the water, then great trouble is threatened.

Books.—This is a good sign, and indicates future happiness, though in a quiet way.

Boots.—You can rely upon the faithfulness of your servants or business employees, if you dream of new and comfortable Boots or Shoes ; but if they are old, or hurt your feet, you will meet with difficulties. (Mod.) Honour and profit. (Anc.)

Borrow.—This is a bad dream, for it foretells domestic

sorrow, not money loss. If you dream that you repay the loan, or that someone repays you, then you will sail into smooth waters once again.

Bottle.—This dream depends upon circumstances. If the Bottle is full, it shows prosperity ; if it is empty, then misfortunes are foretold ; while if you upset the contents, you may expect domestic worries.

Box.—This dream also depends upon the circumstances. If you open a box and find something inside, the dream is fortunate, but if the box is empty, then your plans will be upset.

Boxing Match.—An astonishing announcement will be made in your hearing leading to important events for you. Be wary of repeating or writing about it.

Bride, Bridegroom or Bridesmaids.—Unfortunately this is a dream of contrary. If you are one of these parties, it foretells great disappointment.

Bridge.—To dream that you are crossing a Bridge foretells a change of situation or occupation in business, or a change of district. This will be fortunate if you cross the Bridge without much trouble or delay. If the Bridge is damaged or being repaired, then be careful and do not make any new plans without due thought.

Bread.—If the Bread is new, it is a sign of physical wellbeing. But if it is stale and hard, then domestic worries of a commonplace character are indicated. To bake Bread is an unfortunate omen.

Break.—To damage anything in a dream is a very bad sign, generally concerning the health.

Breath.—To dream that you are out of Breath or exhausted is a warning of coming trouble.

Briars and Brambles.—If they prick you, secret enemies will do you an injury ; if they draw blood, expect heavy losses in trade. If you dream you pass through them without harm, you will triumph over enemies and become happy.

Broom.—Beware of a false friend.

Brother.—See *Relations*.

Bruises.—A warning regarding health. Avoid overstrain.

Brush.—Should you touch or use a brush in your dream, your greatest wish will shortly be granted.

Bubbles.—A sign of gaiety, if they burst trouble will come to you through frivolity.

Buckle.—If it breaks or comes unfastened it betokens difficulty.

Bugle Call.—This announces success in your efforts.

Building.—To dream of Building indicates some change in life, and your success will be the greater if the building is large.

Bull's-eye.—To hit the centre of the target is a lucky dream. If you dream of watching someone else shoot, however, it is a warning of failure.

Burglar.—This signifies treachery amongst those you trust.

Burial.—A dream of contrary denoting a wedding, though not necessarily your own. Burial signifieth wealth. (Anc.)

Burning Houses.—A sign of improved fortunes.

Burns or Scalds.—To Burn yourself in a dream is a sign of a new freindship in your life.

Bushes.—A change is indicated, if you push through them, the change will be for the better.

Butcher.—A sign of an unexpected meeting with someone you have not seen for a long time.

Butter.—This is a good dream, but of a material character, such as feasting. If you are making Butter, some money will reach you unexpectedly.

Butterfly.—A sign of happiness if you see a gaily coloured Butterfly in the sunshine, but if it is a moth, and seen indoors, then it means some slight trouble.

Buttons.—For a man, this is an omen of delay or difficulty in love affairs, but it is fortunate for a woman.

Buy.—To dream that you are buying a lot of articles is a warning of coming troubles in money matters. If, however, you are carefully considering every shilling you spend it is a fortunate sign.

Cabbages.—A sign of health and long life.

Cabin.—To dream that you are in the Cabin of a ship foretells domestic troubles.

Cage.—To dream that you see birds in a Cage is a token of a successful love affair. But if the Cage is empty, the engagement will probably be broken off.

Cake.—Food generally denotes good health, provided it is of an enjoyable kind.

Calendar.—To dream that you are worrying about some date is a sign of a fortunate marriage, unless you fail to find out what you seek.

Calf.—A good omen for lovers and married people.

Calls.—To hear your name called aloud in your dream is fortunate for those in love. It has no money meaning.

Camel.—As with all unusual animals this foretells difficulties and worries.

Camp.—To dream of soldiers in Camp is also fortunate for love affairs, for it is a dream of contrary, and indicates peace in your domestic affairs.

Canary.—A certain sign of a cheerful and comfortable home.

Candle.—This is a good sign, provided the Candle burns brightly. But if it is extinguished, you may expect trouble.

Cap.—If you put on your Cap or Hat in your dream, it signifies difficulty in your love affairs. If a Cap or Hat is given to you, then you will marry happily.

Car, Carriage or Cart.—To dream that you are driving in a Car or other conveyance, is a sign of loss.

Cards.—Signifies deceit and craft. (Anc.)

Cards.—Playing at Cards in a dream, or watching other people play, is an indication of coming quarrels. (Mod.)

Carpenter.—To see workmen busily engaged, is a sign that you will overcome your difficulties.

Carpet.—To dream that you are in a room containing a handsome Carpet, is a fortunate dream.

Carrots.—This dream signifies profit by inheritance.

Carving.—This dream depends upon the circumstances. If you are serving yourself, it shows your own prosperity, but if you are Carving for other people, then someone else will benefit by your actions.

Castle.—This omen is generally held to indicate a quarrel through your own bad temper.

Cat.—An unfavourable dream, which shows unexpected deceit by someone whom you trust. The ancient meaning runs as follows :—" If any one dreams that he hath encountered a Cat or killed one, he will commit a thief to prison and prosecute him to the death, for the Cat signifies a common thief."

Caterpillars.—To dream you see Caterpillars signifies ill-luck and misfortune from secret enemies. (Anc.)

Cattle.—A sign of prosperity in business, but if you see yourself driving Cattle, it shows that you have to work hard. Black Cattle, however, show trouble in business, owing to the unfortunate colour.

Ceiling.—A dream of warning ; if the Ceiling cracks or falls, it presages coming illness.

Cellar.—If filled with coal, a good business omen ; otherwise it means obstacles to success.

Cemetery.—You will conquer all things.

Chains.—A dream of contrary, showing that you will escape from some difficulty that is worrying you at the moment. But a gold Chain round a woman's neck shows good fortune from some friend or lover.

Chair.—To see an empty Chair in your dream, indicates news from a long absent friend.

Chalk.—To dream of Chalk cliffs means disappointment in some cherished hopes.

Cheese.—To dream that you eat Cheese signifies profit and gain. (Anc.)

Chickens.—To dream of a hen and her chickens signifies loss and damage. (Anc.)

Children.— A lucky dream, showing success in business.

Chimney.—To see a tall Chimney predicts fortunate events.

China.—Financial gain from a long distance.

Choking.—Strangely enough, it is a fortunate dream to find yourself Choking in your dream.

Christening.—This dream has also to do with the interior of a sacred building ; it is not a fortunate omen.

Christmas.—A good omen, but it refers more particularly to your friends or family affairs, and not to business.

Church.—Here again it is the outside of the building that is fortunate. To dream that you are in the inside of a sacred building is a warning of coming trouble.

Churchyard.—Although apparently unpleasant, this is a fortunate dream, as it concerns the outside of a Church.

Churning.—To dream that you are Churning is a sign of prosperity and plenty ; to the single, happy marriage.

Cider.—Gossip about your own private affairs. Act cautiously.

Cigarette.—To dream you are lighting one signifies new plans ; a half-smoked Cigarette, held in the hand, is a postpone-ment ; to smoke it to the end, means a successful conclusion to your hopes.

Cinders.—Ashes or Cinders in a dream are a bad sign—expect disappointment.

Circus.– A sign of future unhappiness, due to your own careless habits.

City.—A large City denotes ambition, if in the distance, successfully attained should you enter it in your dream.

Clergyman.—Strictly speaking, this is a dream of dis-appointment. It concerns the inside of a church, which is never a fortunate omen.

Climbing.—It is a sign of business prosperity to find your-self Climbing, unless the effort proves too great for your strength. Still, even then, it shows some sort of good fortune, though combined with difficulties.

Cliffs.—A dangerous dream. Do not take any risks, espe-cially of high places from which you might slip, for some time.

Clock.—To dream that you hear a Clock strike the hours is a fortunate sign. You will enjoy a comfortable life.

Clothes.—This is a dream of contrary—if you have plenty of Clothes in your dream, it is a warning of coming trouble. If you are partly dressed or naked, then prosperity is coming your way. To put on Clothes is a fortunate sign, but depends a great deal on the colour of the Clothes. See *Colours*.

Clouds.—This dream depends upon the circumstances; if the sky is stormy and dark, it betokens many troubles. But if the Clouds pass away, then better fortunes await you.

Cobwebs.—To brush them away signifies triumph.

Coffin.—Signifies the illness of a dear friend.

Colours.—If you dream about Flags, Decorations or Clothes in many bright colours, it signifies prosperity and success in all your undertakings. WHITE is always favourable, especially in matters concerning other people. BLACK is the sinister colour, unless you dream of a funeral, in which case it is appropriate and signifies only a struggle before success. BLUE and PURPLE represent prosperity through other people, good fortune in your love affairs and so on. SCARLET or RED is a warning of quarrels, the loss of friends; but CRIMSON denotes pleasant news from an unexpected quarter. YELLOW and ORANGE are mental tints and show that you need not expect any important change in your affairs for some time. GREEN indicates a journey, or business with people at a distance.

Combing.—To dream that you are Combing your hair, or that of some other person, is a sign of loss through deceit.

Command.—To dream you see one Command signifieth anger. (Anc.)

Coppers.—These are luckiest when you dream of bestowing them upon someone else; given to you, they signify loss.

Cord.—To knot a Cord means the strengthening of a friendship; to unravel it means the breaking of an engagement.

Confections.—To dream of sweetmeats betokens pleasure. (Anc.)

Corks.—If you dream that you are extracting a Cork, it is a sign of some good news of a friend.

Corkscrew.—It is a sign of illness to use a Corkscrew in your dream.

Corn or Cornfield.—A very fortunate dream and a sign of money in plenty according to the state of the growing corn.

Corns.—To dream that you have Corns on your feet is a sign of fortunate business ventures.

Corpse.—An omen of estrangement or separation from friends through your own fault; an unhappy love affair.

Cottage.—It is a fortunate sign to find yourself living in a Cottage, unless you are discontented and endeavour to get away.

Coughing.—This is a dream of contrary and indicates good health, vigour and business prosperity.

Crab.—Beware of the law.

Cradle.—It is not a good sign to dream of an empty Cradle ; misfortune will come, probably through ill health.

Cross.—An omen of sorrow in the affections.

Cross Roads.—To the unmarried, an engagement will soon be made, either by you or among your friends.

Crow.—The sinister omen, Black, makes this bird an omen of grief and misfortune. If more than one Crow is seen, the matter becomes very serious.

Crowds.—Your happiness is assured and will increase.

Crown.—To dream of having a Crown of gold on your head, signifies the friendship of your employer, and the dreamer will be honoured by many persons and have many gifts. (Anc.)

Crumbs.—To dream of birds pecking at Crumbs, foretells both gifts and good tidings.

Crutches.—This is an obstacle dream—if you recover and are able to walk without the aid of the Crutches, all will go well. If not, expect trouble.

Crystal.—You will soon be shown the " turning " in the " long lane " that has been worrying you.

Cuckoo.—A dream signifying misfortune in love affairs or in the married state.

Cup.—An empty Cup is a bad omen, but a full one is a sign of prosperity.

Cupboard.—To dream of an empty Cupboard is a bad sign for your business prosperity. If you put things inside, it shows you will recover your losses after some distress.

Curls.—A complete change in your affairs ; new environment, and better times in view.

Curse.—To dream of hearing Curses and rough language, presages a visit of ceremony.

Curtain.—This is an obstacle dream, but refers particularly to deceit in someone you trust. If you pull the Curtain aside, you will be warned in time.

Cushion.—Signs of comfort in your dreams are not fortunate ; the more comfortable you find yourself, the greater will be your difficulties and business worries.

Cutlery.—Small vexations and annoyances.

Cuttle-fish.—A very grave warning of personal danger.

Cyclamen.—All dreams of flowers are good unless they appear to be faded, when they are a sign of hopes beyond your reach.

Cycling.—A sign of some event postponed. Do not try to hurry things, you will be successful in the long run.

Cypress.—This denotes bad news of one who is dear to you.

D

Dairy.—A fortunate dream. See *Butter*.

Dance or Dancing.—To dream of Dancing is a sign that money is coming to you, or that a cherished plan will succeed. To watch dancing, signifies that you will hear of a friend's good fortune.

Danger.—This is one of contrary. Facing Danger in your dream, you may expect success ; if you avoid it, then trouble will come.

Darkness.—To dream that you are in the Dark is a sign of difficulties ahead, but if you succeed in groping your way to the light, you will overcome them successfully.

Darning.—To dream you are Darning, denotes the introduction of a new friend. To see it, is a warning against gossip.

The Dead.—To dream of the Dead means news of the living. To speak to, is a sign of long life. To touch or kiss, means sorrow. (Mod.) Signifies courage and a clear conscience. (Anc.)

Dentist.—Sickness and ill-health.

Desert.—To dream that you are crossing a Desert, signifies difficulties concerning some cherished plan.

Desk.—This dream depends upon whether the Desk is open or closed. If closed and locked, bad news will follow. If sitting at an open desk, you will have good news.

Devil.—This is a very bad dream if you imagine you see Satan, but the outcome depends on circumstances. It always means a long struggle.

Diamonds.—To find them, means trouble ; to sell, coming danger.

Dice.—Playing with Dice is a sign of changing fortunes, but circumstances may alter the results.

Digging.—Good fortune if the ground is dry, finding money, and good fortune if the amount is a large one.

Ditch.—All obstacles of a material kind are bad signs ; beware of unexpected difficulties, especially in money matters.

Diving.—To dream that you are Diving or falling into water is a sign of loss of money in speculation, or in some risky business undertaking.

Drink.—If you dream that you are thirsty and cannot find water it shows misfortune. If the water is dirty or muddy it is a bad sign, as also if it is warm or hot. But to Drink clear, fresh water in a very good sign. It is also fortunate to Drink milk. (Mod.) To drink wine signifies health. (Anc.)

Driving.—It is a fortunate dream if someone else is Driving you ; but if you yourself are the Driver, then expect money losses.

Doctor.—A good omen ; fortune and health, a rise in life.

Dog.—(howling) danger ; (to lose one) misfortune ; (to hunt with one) hopefulness ; (to play with one) suffering from former wastefulness ; (two fighting) false friends.

Donkey.—Quarrelsome friends ; (asleep) security ; (braying) dishonour ; (heavily laden) profit ; (to shoe one) hard and useless labour.

Dove.—Happiness in domestic affairs.

Dragon.—To see one, great riches.

Draughts or Chess.—A somewhat similar dream to Dice. It shows fluctuations of fortunes, and you should avoid all speculative business or betting.

Drums.—It is a fortunate omen to hear Drums in a dream and denotes success.

Ducks or Geese.—A good sign. If the Geese attack you, it means trouble in business affairs.

Dust.—Dust or Dirt is a bad omen, and shows struggle against adverse circumstances. To dream that you are Dusting a room means that some improvement will come if you persevere.

Dwarf.—If you see a Dwarf in your dream, it is a sign of difficulties in your domestic circle.

Dye.—To dream you are Dyeing your hair or rouging your cheeks is a bad sign. You will suffer through your own folly.

Dynamite.—This is a warning of serious danger to either business or domestic affairs.

E

Eagle.—(flying) ambition and gratified fortune ; (dead) loss. (Anc.)

Ear-rings.—This omen in a dream signifies a quarrel. It does not matter whether you wear them, give them to someone or receive them as a present.

Ears.—To dream of any trouble with your Ears is a bad sign—it shows trouble from some unexpected source.

Eat.—To Eat lard or salt signifies a murmuring ; to Eat

cheese signifies gain and profit ; to Eat apples signifies anger. (Anc.)

Eclipse.—(sun) misfortune ; (moon) success.

Eels.—(alive) hard work ; (dead) triumph over enemies.

Eggs.—To dream of Eggs signifies gain and profit, especially to physicians, painters and those who sell and trade with them. To dream you see broken Eggs is a very bad sign and signifies loss to the party dreaming. (Anc.)

Elephant.—This friendly beast denotes assistance from friends or outside influences.

Embroidery.—Affection which is returned.

Entertainment.—This dream depends upon the circumstances. It is usually a very fortunate omen, unless for any reason you feel uncomfortable. If you leave before the Entertainment is over, it is a sign that you will miss some good opportunity through your own carelessness.

Escape.—This is a straight dream which depends upon the apparent happenings. If you Escape from any difficulty in your dream, it means success in your personal affairs, a triumph over difficulties. If you Escape from fire or water, you may expect anxious moments, but a successful issue ; if from some wild animal, then look for treachery near you. If in your dream you do not Escape, then it is a very bad sign.

Evil Spirits.—A very serious omen unless you succeed in driving them away. Be careful in your business.

Ewe.—A large family and prosperous times to come.

Examination.—An obstacle dream. If you find that the Examination is too difficult, then expect business worries. If, however, you can answer most of the questions and dream that you are doing well, then some unexpected good fortune awaits you.

Exchange.—If you dream that you are exchanging articles with some other person, expect business losses and difficulties.

Excursion.—Be on your guard against a married associate who may not be a true friend.

Execution.—The success of your undertakings will be doubtful.

Exhibition.—This is not a good omen, signifying difficulties ahead, but you will be able to overcome them with patience.

Explosion.—This denotes news of ill fortune to either a relative or close friend.

Express.—If you dream of travelling in one beware of offending those above you in business ; if you see one passing, you will hear of danger to a friend.

Eyeglass.—This betokens good news of a fortunate business matter.

Eyelids.—An omen of trouble among those around you. Watch carefully and help if you can.

Eyes.—It is considered fortunate to see strange eyes staring at you in your dream. Some important change will soon take place. But if you are worried about your own eyes, then be careful in your actions for someone is working secretly against you.

F

Fable.—To read or hear Fables is a happy omen of an end to your worries and vexations.

Fabulous Creatures.—To dream of any strange animals or Fabulous Creatures is far from good, but should they not attempt to attack you it is only a warning of troubles which may happen if you are not watchful.

Face.—To dream you see a fresh, taking, smiling Face and countenance is a sign of friendship and joy. To dream you see faces of absolute strangers shows a change of residence or of occupation. (Anc.)

Factory.—A Factory is a sign of some unexpected happening.

Faggots.—Bad news.

Failure.—This is a dream of contrary, since if you fail in any attempt in your dream, you will succeed in real life.

Fairies.—This is a very favourable dream and shows success when least expected.

Fairs.—It is not fortunate to dream that you are present at a fair.

Falcon.—Good fortune attained by your own efforts.

Farm.—To dream that you are engaged in Farm work is a fortunate omen ; it indicates material success, though after some struggle on your part. If you only visit a Farm it indicates good health.

Father.—If in your dream you see your Father, and he speaks to you, it is a sign of coming happiness. If he is silent or if he appears to be ill or dead, then you may expect trouble. See also *Mother*.

Father-in-law.—To dream you see your Father-in-law, either dead or alive, signifies ill-luck, especially if he uses violence or is threatening.

Fatigue.—(yourself) success in business.

Fawn.—Dangers to come soon.

Feast.—Trouble in store.

Feathers.—(white) friendship and happiness ; (black) losses.

Fence.—(climbing) a sudden rise in life ; (creeping under) a warning to avoid shady transactions.

Fields.—Family joy and good health. (Anc.)

Figs.—(dried) rejoicings ; (green) hope ; (to eat) ill fortunes to be expected. (Mod.) Signifies joy and pleasure. (Anc.)

Fire.—Quarrels ; (small) good news.

Fish.—Success ; (to catch them) your friends are false ; (dead) quarrels ana disappointments.

Fleas.—Weariness of life ; (to kill one) success over enemies.

Flies.—Good fortune excites jealousy.

Floating.—(On water) good fortune and speedy success ; (sinking) look out for reverses of fortune.

Flowers.—Happiness. (To gather) abiding friendship ; (to cast away) quarrels.

Flute.—(To hear) news of a birth.

Footman.—Unexpected enemies.

Forest.—Misfortune and disgrace.

Fountain.—A good dream ; prosperity and health.

Fox.—(killed) good ; (petted) danger ; (to see one) secret enemies.

Friend.—Quarrels made up.

Fright.—To be interpreted by its contrary.

Frogs.—Deceitfulness ; (hopping) vexation and annoyance ; (catching) good fortune. (Mod.) Signify flatterers. (Anc.)

Fruit.—To dream of Fruit has a different interpretation according to what the Fruit is ; Apples show long life and success ; a boy to a woman with child ; cheerfulness in your sweetheart and riches in trade ; Cherries indicate disappointment in love and vexation in the married state. (Anc.)

Funeral.—This dream is associated with the colour Black, but if you see yourself present at a Funeral in Black it is appropriate, so no trouble need be expected. It is a dream of contrary and indicates a successful love affair.

Funeral Service.—Inheritance.

Fur or Fur Garments.—A favourable dream on the whole, though it foretells change of some sort.

Furnace.—This is an omen very similar to forge in its meaning.

Furniture.—This is generally a good dream, but it depends upon circumstances. Handsome Furniture is very fortunate, but naturally this depends upon the person who dreams. What is ordinary Furniture for a wealthy woman would be sheer folly for a working-class woman, or for a business girl earning her own living.

G

Garden.—A very fortunate dream. Nature at her best, but of course it must be a garden that is well kept and not neglected. It concerns money matters.

Garland.—Anticipated pleasures will be realised. **See** *Flowers.*

Garlic or Onions.—These are generally considered fortunate omens. But there are many people who detest the smell of onions; in such cases they should be regarded as signs of ill-success.

Gauze.—Concealed feelings.

Geese.—To dream you hear them cackling signifies success. (Anc.)

Gift.—A dream of contrary—beware of the person from whom you receive a gift under such circumstances.

Gloves.—Modern meaning—transient joy ; ancient meaning—if wearing gloves, honour and safety.

Goat.—(White) good fortune ; (black) illness ; (on high places) riches.

Gold.—A dream of contrary as far as the metal itself is concerned, for it signifies loss of money. But if your clothes are of Gold cloth, or if they are embroidered with Gold ornamentation, it is a good sign. Ancient meaning—" To dream one hath a crown of Gold upon his head signifies favour with his sovereign and that he shall be honoured and feared by many. For a man to dream that he hath found Gold, and cannot tell where to hide it, or that he is afraid to be taken with it, shows he shall have a wife who shall rob his purse and take away all his money while he is asleep. (Anc.)

Grapes.—To dream of eating Grapes at any time signifies cheerfulness and profit. To tread Grapes signifies the overthrow of enemies. To gather white Grapes signifies gain, but to dream of gathering black Grapes signifies damage. (Anc.) (To eat) good fortune ; (to throw away) loss ; (to tread on) plenty. (Mod.)

Grave.—News from afar. If the Grave space is open, the news will not be good.

Grinding.—(Corn) good fortune ; (coffee) trouble at home ; (pepper) sickness and sorrow.

Grindstone.—To be using a Grindstone in your dreams is an omen of contrary—good fortune will attend your efforts.

Guitar or Banjo.—This is much the same omen as Violin and is a fortunate dream if you hear it played, but signifies ill-news if you play it yourself.

Gulf.—A sign of a parting which will sadden you, but which may be avoided if you are careful.

Gum.—Someone will " stick to you " in an emergency, financial difficulties are indicated.

Gun.—To hear the report of a Gun is an omen of illness to one who is dear to you, but if you fire the Gun yourself it is a sign of trouble coming to you.

Gunpowder.—A sign of a speedy change of residence.

Gutter.—To dream of finding something valuable in the Gutter is a sign of financial reward coming to you for work well done, but to dream of being in the Gutter yourself signifies poverty.

Gymnasium.—To dream of exercising in a Gymnasium is a good dream if you seem to be vigorous and enjoying the exercise ; but should you feel tired it is a warning that you are attempting some enterprise which cannot possibly succeed.

H

Habit.—To dream of putting on or wearing a Habit, indicates a great effort which you will have to make to escape from an unhappy position.

Haddock.—Most dreams of fish are fortunate.

Hag.—To see a Hag or witch forebodes scandal, but if she speaks to or touches you, your reputation is in danger from the spite of jealous tongues. Guard your speech and actions.

Hail.—To dream of Hail signifies sorrow and trouble, and sometimes that the most hidden secrets shall be revealed and made known. (Anc.) Affliction and sorrow. (Mod.)

Ham.—Joy and pleasure.

Hands.—(Tied) troubles.

Hare.—(Running) fortune leaving you.

Hat.—To dream that your Hat is broken or fallen off means damage and dishonour. (Anc.)

Hay.—Happiness and success ; (to mow it) sorrow.

Hell.—To dream of descending into Hell and returning thence, to those who are rich, signifies misfortune, but it is a good sign to the poor and weak. (Anc.)

Hen.—Substantial profit ; (cackling) immense fortune ; (with chicks) doubtful fortune ; (laying eggs) gain.

Herbs.—Good fortune will be yours ; (to eat) disappointment.

Holly.—Vexation and disagreements.

Honey.—Profitable enterprises.

Horse.—Success ; (black) partial success only ; (white) very good fortune ; (to shoe one) very lucky.

Horseman.—A dangerous journey.

Hunger.—To dream one is extraordinarily hungry and that his appetite craves sustenance, shows that he will be ingenious, laborious and eager in getting an estate and that he will grow rich in proportion to the greatness of his Hunger. (Anc.)

Husband.—An omen of contrary, for if you dream you are married when you are not, then expect a quarrel with one dear to you.

Hymns.—To dream that you are singing Hymns is a fortunate omen ; your plans will be very successful.

Hysterics.—To see any one hysterical is a warning against being persuaded to act against your wishes. To dream of being in Hysterics warns the dreamer to profit by good advice from those who wish him well.

I

Ice.—This is always an unfortunate dream ; expect many difficulties.

Illness.—A warning of some great temptation that will not work out favourably for you, however promising it appears at first.

Injury.—To dream that you have been Injured by someone shows that you have a rival, in business or love, who will prove a danger to you.

Ink.—(spilled) separation and losses.

Insects.—The interpretation of a dream concerning Insects depends upon the circumstances. If the Insects fly or crawl away from you, it is considered that a disappointment awaits the dreamer in his business affairs.

Iron.—For one to dream that he sees himself hurt with an Iron, signifies that he shall receive some damage. To dream that one trades with a stranger in Iron, signifies to the dreamer losses and misfortune. (Anc.) Most metals indicate difficulties when they are prominent in a dream, but the colour may be held to affect this. Silver or gold would carry the significance of White or Yellow, whereas Iron would be similar to Black. (Mod.)

Ironing.—A change for the better. Keep yourself free from ties and responsibilities for a time. Help will come to you in an unexpected way.

Ivory.—A very fortunate dream when Ivory is concerned.

Ivy.—Good health awaits you, unless the Ivy is pulled away from its support.

J

Jack.—To dream of playing cards and holding the Jack of Clubs, a good friend, of Diamonds a false friend, of Hearts, a true lover, of Spades, an enemy.

Jackal.—Some enemy will backbite you and cause you trouble.

Jackass.—A good omen as regards love affairs.

Jackdaw.—An omen of difficulties, unless the bird is in a cage or you catch it.

Jade.—To dream of green indicates hard mental work to come, but ornaments signify success, so your work will be well rewarded.

Jail.—An unfortunate dream unless you dream of being released from one.

Jars.—An omen of plenty if full, but of want if empty.

Jet.—An omen of mourning.

Jewels.—Always a very fortunate dream, especially for lovers.

Jockey.—An omen of luck in love, especially if he is riding at full speed.

Joint.—To dream of cooking a lean Joint is a sign of poverty, but to cook a fat Joint for other people and not eat of it yourself is an omen of wealth to come.

Journey.—A change in your circumstances is shown, but the details of the Journey will show the result. If your voyage is a pleasant one, all will be for the best, but if the road is rough or the weather stormy guard your actions.

Judge.—An obstacle dream denoting troubles and difficulties to be encountered.

Juggler.—An advancement in position will come within your grasp. Do not hesitate to take it.

Jugs.—It is a favourable omen if you break a Jug in your dream.

Jumping.—Another of the many obstacle dreams. If you Jump safely in your dream you will overcome the difficulties.

Jungle.—As with dreams of wild animals this is not a favourable omen, but if you escape from the Jungle you will overcome your obstacles.

Juniper.—This presages evil speaking, guard your tongue and your actions for a time.

Jury.—To see the Jury in court is a favourable omen, but not if you form one of a Jury yourself.

K

Kettle.—A very happy omen if the Kettle is clean, but look out for troubles and losses if the water boils over.

Key.—A Key seen in a dream to him who would marry, signifies a handsome wife and good housekeeper. (Anc.) For the married, increase in business. To dream that you lose a Key is a bad sign. (Mod.)

Kill.—To dream of killing a man signifies success in business ; but to dream that you are being killed denotes loss to him who kills you. (Anc.)

King.—To dream of your sovereign ruler is a sign of difficulties which can be overcome by hard work. Keep at it and all will go well.

Kiss.—Awakening affecton.

Kitchen.—Visit from relatives.

Kite.—This omen depends upon the circumstances. If the Kite flies easily, you may expect success, and the higher up it goes, the better the omen. (Anc.)

Kitten.—A favourable dream unless you hurt the young creature.

Knife.—Quarrels with friends that will lead to much misfortune. (Anc.)

Knitting.—Your undertakings will be crowned with success. If you see someone Knitting you will be deceived.

Knocking.—You are well on the way to happiness, but guard your speech in the next few days as your temper will be tested.

Knots.—A foreboding of as many worries as there are Knots in your dress, but if you unravel the Knots it is less serious.

Knuckles.—To dream of knocking with your Knuckles at a closed door is a sign of unreturned affections.

L

Label.—To dream of tying Labels on to luggage is a portent of a long and successful journey to be taken speedily.

Laboratory.—This is an omen of danger and sickness.

Labourer.—Increased wealth.

Lace.—A dream of contrary—the more a woman is decked out in your dream the greater the coming trouble.

Ladder.—Climbing up a Ladder is a good sign, but the reverse is an indication of troubles ahead of you. (Anc.) The number of rungs should be noted, for this increases the power of the omen. To feel dizzy on a ladder is always a bad sign. (Mod.)

Lambs.—(to find one) success at law ; (in fields) peacefulness and health ; (to eat) sorrow.

Lame Man.—Business difficulties.

Lamps.—Showiness.

Land.—You will triumph over your enemies.

Landscape.—Great good fortune.

Lantern.—This is usually a fortunate omen, but the light must be good. It it is dim, or if it goes out altogether, then expect worries and difficulties. (Anc.)

Larks.—You will soon be richer than you are.

Laughter.—Grief and pain.

Laurel.—Pleasure and profitable undertakings.

Lawyer.—The marriage of a friend.

Leaf or Leaves.—To see trees in full Leaf in your dream is a very happy omen. Your affairs will prosper. Nature is favourable. It is a very good dream for lovers, especially if blossom is seen in addition to the Leaf. With Fruit, it is a sign of a happy marriage. But if the Leaves are withered or are falling as in Autumn, it shows loss in business, disappointment in love and domestic affairs, quarrels with friends.

Leather.—It is an unfortunate omen when you dream of Leather in any form, whether as a strap, a bag, harness or anything else.

Leech.—Fortunate. Friends and happiness await you.

Leeks.—Perseverance in your project will bring its reward in due time.

Leopard.—Dangers and travels.

Letters.—(To receive) good news from abroad.

Lettuce.—Misfortune is awaiting you.

Light.—When one dreams that one holds a burning Light in one's hand it is a good sign, and chiefly to those who are young, for it signifies that they shall prosper in love, accomplish their designs, overcome their enemies, and gain honour and good will from all persons. To dream you see a burning Light in the hands of another, signifies that the mischief done will be discovered and the party punished. (Anc.)

Lightning.—A love squabble.

Lily.—Happiness and prosperity await you, but only as the result of your own industry.

Linen.—To dream that you are dressed in clean Linen is a favourable sign ; you may expect good news before long. (Anc.) If your Linen is soiled or stained, it denotes serious loss in business, unless you see yourself change the garment, when you may expect to get over your worst difficulties. A dream of Linen also depends upon the colour of the garment. See *Colour*. (Mod.)

Lion.—This dream is not the same in significance as if you see a Leopard. The Lion signifies some purely personal honour or success, not necessarily involving a gain of money. But if you hear the Lion roaring as if angry, then expect some misfortune through the jealousy of someone near to you. A Lion Cub is a sign of a valuable friendship. (Mod.) To fight one signifies a quarrel. (Anc.)

Lioness.—Dreaming of seeing a Lioness is good to rich and poor.

Lizard.—Treachery.

Lobster.—A favourable omen for your love affairs or your domestic happiness.

Locks.—This is another obstacle dream and you will encounter difficulties in the near future. If cabinets or drawers are locked and you cannot find the keys, it is a bad sign, and you should be very careful in money matters and avoid speculation or risk of any kind. If later you find the keys, you will pull through, but even then it should be taken as a warning.

Lodgings.—To dream you are hunting for Lodgings signifies delay in a matter of importance.

Logs.—Logs of wood or the fallen trunks of trees are favourable omens in your dreams ; but you must not interfere with them or cut them up.

Logs.—To dream that one is cleaving of Logs is a sign that strangers shall come to the house. (Anc.)

Looking or Looking-glass.—To dream of Looking down from high places, or out of windows, or being in a high garret, shows an ambitious mind, curious desires, wandering imagination and confused thoughts. To dream of Looking in a Glass to married folks, betokens children. (Anc.)

Lord.—To dream you discourse with a Lord, or that you go into any place with him, signifies honour. (Anc.)

Lost and Losing.—For a woman to dream that she has Lost her wedding-ring signifies danger of Losing her husband's affection. For a man to dream of losing things denotes that he will meet with reproaches. (Anc.) To dream that you have Lost your shoes or some other important article of clothing is very unfortunate, for your troubles will be due to your own attempts at being too clever. (Mod.)

Love.—This is a dream of contrary as far as sweethearts are concerned. To dream that you do not succeed in Love is a sign that you will marry and have a happy life. But to dream that your friends are fond of you is a very fortunate omen and indicates prosperity. To dream that you are in the company of your Lover is also fortunate.

Luggage.—A dream that signifies difficulties in your path, though it depends upon the quantity of the Luggage you have with you and whether you are able to deal with it successfully.

For the lover it foretells quarrels, slight or important, according to circumstances.

Lumber.—Trouble and misfortune.

Lunatic.—Surprising news.

Luxury.—A dream of contrary meaning poverty to come.

Lying.—To dream of telling or of discovering lies is a sign of a false friend.

Lynx.—As with all unusual creatures, this is not a good omen, but if the creature does not attack you it is less unfortunate.

M

Mackerel.—Deceit and evil tidings.

Machinery.—This dream depends upon whether you feel interested in the Machinery; if so, it is a favourable sign, though it means hard work. But if you feel afraid of the Machinery, then be careful in your ventures, for you will surely fail to carry out your purpose.

Magic.—To dream of things happening by supernatural and unknown means is a sign that changes are coming in your affairs, through some unexpected source. The ultimate result, fortunate or otherwise, will depend upon the details of your dream, but as a rule, the result will be beneficial. But the unexpected happening may mean the loss of a friend, or some event that appears at the time to be unfortunate.

Mantle or Cloak.—Be warned of treachery on the part of someone whom you trust.

Manure.—To dream that you are cultivating the soil is a good sign for those in subordinate positions, but it is not so fortunate for the wealthy. (Anc.)

Marriage or Marrying.—To dream that you witness a Marriage is a warning of ill-health. But if you assist at the ceremony it shows some pleasing news but not of great importance. To dream that you are being married, either as Bride or Bridegroom, is a most unfortunate omen. (Mod.) Sickness and Death. (Anc.)

Mason.—To dream that you are building a house or employ someone to do it for you, is a sign of loss due to illness; it is a very unfortunate dream. (Anc.)

Medlars.—Your enjoyment will cease and trouble ensue.

Melon.—Satisfaction.

Metals.—To dream of Gold indicates trouble ahead, but there will be no immediate change. You will have time to put things right. To dream of Silver indicates a disappointment in love that will not prove as unpleasant as you anticipate. To dream of Copper coins, is an indication of small but vexatious worries.

Mice.—An indication of trouble through a friend or a business associate.

Mills.—Inheritance of fortune by a legacy.

Mirror.—False friends ; (broken) the death of a relative.

Misfortune.—This is a dream of contrary. If you dream that some Misfortune happens to yourself or to someone you love, it shows some fortunate stroke of business that will result in a far greater success than you expect.

Money.—To dream that you pay or give Money to other people is a fortunate omen ; prosperity awaits you. To dream that you receive Money also foretells personal success, but due to hard work. To find Money in your dream is not so fortunate, however, there will be some sudden advancement or success, but it will prove disappointing.

Moon.—This dream depends upon the circumstances. If the Moon is bright and shines clearly, free from cloud, it foretells success in love, personal happiness. If the Moon is clouded over, it shows ill-health or some other interruption to your comfort and enjoyment. A New Moon is fortunate for business, a Full Moon for love affairs.

Motor Car.—If you are riding in one, new surroundings are portended.

Mountain.—Another dream indicating obstacles in your path—the ultimate result depends upon the circumstance. If you climb to the top, all will go well, though it means hard work, as unexpected difficulties will confront you. (Mod.) Fear and trouble. (Anc.)

Mourning.—A dream of contrary. Great prosperity is before you if you are a business man, or married happiness if you are a lover.

Movies.—Frivolous invitations ; do not trust fair women.

Moving or Removal.—It is not a fortunate dream to see your furniture being removed from one house to another.

Mule.—To dream of a mule signifies malice and folly. (Anc.)

Music.—To dream you hear melodious music signifies acceptable news with which he shall be delighted. (Anc.) Pleasures in store. (Mod.)

N

Nails.—To dream your Nails are grown long is very good, and denotes riches, prosperity, and happiness, and great success in love, a good industrious husband or wife, and dutiful children.

It also foretells that you will suddenly receive a sum of money that will be of great use to you. (Anc.)

Navigating a Vessel.—You will take a long journey.

Neck.—To dream of the Neck signifies power, honour, riches and inheritance. (Anc.)

Necklace.—Jealousy and quarrels.

Needles.—Disappointments in love.

Negro.—Spiteful friends.

Nettles.—To dream of Nettles and that you sting yourself with them shows that you will venture hard for what you desire to obtain. (Anc.)

Nest.—Good fortune and prosperity.

Night-Birds.—To dream of any sort of Night-Birds, as the owlet, the great owl, bittern and bat, ominious ; and Ansalmous Julius advises those who have such dreams to undertake no business on the day following. (Anc.)

Nightingale.—To dream of this pretty warbler is the fore-runner of joyful news, great success in business, plentiful crops and of a sweet tempered lover. (Anc.)

Noises.—Your position will be influenced by someone dying.

Nosegay.—To dream of gathering and making Nosegays is unlucky, showing that your best hopes shall wither as flowers do in a Nosegay. To dream of garlands is very good in the Spring but bad in the other seasons. (Anc.)

Nurse.—A good omen.

Nuts.—Your wishes will be gratified.

Nut Trees.—To dream that you see Nut Trees and that you crack and eat their fruit, signifies riches and content, gained with labour and pains. To dream that you find nuts that have been hidden signifies that you will find some treasure. (Anc.)

O

Oak.—Prosperity and long life ; (felled) losses. Riches. (Anc.)

Oil.—To dream that you are using Oil in any way is an unfortunate omen, except for women or those who use it normally, such as artists, painters or contractors and the like. (Anc.)

Old Man.—Good fortune.

Old Woman.—Scandal.

Olives.—A good omen. (Mod.) Olive Tree, peace and happiness. (Anc.)

Onions.—(peeling) family troubles ; (eating) unexpected good fortune. (Mod.) A mixture of good and ill-luck. (Anc.)

Opera.—Enjoyment which is not without its penalties.

Orange Blossom.—A near marriage.

Oranges.—Amusement; (to eat) pleasures to come.

Orchard.—To dream that you are in an Orchard is always a favourable sign, but the actual extent of your good fortune will depend upon the condition of the fruit. If it is ripe and plentiful, you may expect great success. If it is green and scarce then your fortunes will mend, but it will require time and patience.

Orchestra.—Music is generally considered a fortunate omen in a dream, but in the case of an Orchestra there will be too many difficulties and failure generally results.

Organ.—(solemn music) sickness and family troubles. (Mod.) Joy. (Anc.)

Ornaments.—A dream of contrary. The more Ornaments you wear in your dream, the greater will be the coming trouble.

Ostler.—To dream of stablemen or anything to do with horses is a good omen; you are in favour with Fortune and will have luck in all undertakings.

Oven.—To dream that you are baking or cooking some food in an Oven is a sign that your affairs have reached a standstill. If you burn the food you will drift slowly to the bad; if the result is a pleasant meal, then in time you will prosper.

Oxen.—To dream that you see a herd of Oxen is a very fortunate sign; your affairs will prosper. If they are grazing peacefully, your speculations or investments should be watched as they should show signs of favourable development. Buy and sell shares carefully.

Oysters.—Denotes hunger which the dreamer shall sustain. (Anc.)

P

Painter.—A good dream, especially if at work outside the house.

Painting.—Domestic affliction.

Palm Tree.—You will be successful in your enterprises and confound those who oppose you. (Anc.)

Paper.—To dream of Paper is a sign of some coming trouble. If the Paper is clean you will escape with a slight money loss. But if the Paper is soiled and dirty, then your own questionable action will prove your undoing. If the Paper is folded it denotes some small disappointment.

Parent.—Success for one you hold dear.

Parrot.—Hard work is before you; you will suffer from the idle talk of other people.

Parsley.—Like most green things this is an omen of success that has been achieved by hard work.

Parsnip.—Subjection to a master is denoted.

Pastry.—This is a very similar dream and is a warning that you should move carefully both in business and in love.

Peach.—A dream of personal pleasure, not of business affairs.

Peaches.—Content, health and pleasure. (Anc.)

Peacock.—A dream of contrary—your fine plans will fail and you will be disappointed. But to the farmer this handsome bird foretells a good harvest after much hard work.

Pearls.—A very favourable dream, but you will have to earn your success by hard work. Be patient, for you will surely succeed. If Pearls are given to you in your dream it is a sign of a very happy and successful marriage. If the string of Pearls should break, however, it shows grief and sorrow unless you should thread them again in your dream.

Peas.—This is a fortunate dream on the whole, but you must exercise patience, particularly if the peas are raw or not cooked sufficiently. It is most favourable when you see the Peas growing in the garden. Dried Peas show money, but acquired in a doubtful manner. (Anc.)

Pens.—News about absent friends.

Pheasant.—Good fortune ; (to carry one) honours.

Pictures.—To dream one draws Pictures is pleasure without profit. (Anc.)

Pigeons.—News of importance from afar, but it may not be very favourable. It will mean changes in your affairs. They are favourable in love affairs and it is better to see them flying in the air than walking on the ground or settling on ledges.

Pigs.—A very mixed dream, for good and bad luck will both be present in your affairs. Many of your cherished plans will fail, yet others, apparently less important, will succeed and restore the balance. Watch over the members of your household as trouble may reach you from this source.

Pilgrim.—This dream promises the fulfilment of a great wish.

Pin Cushion.—It is a favourable sign if there are plenty of pins stuck in the Cushion. If not, then expect disappointment.

Pine Tree.—This signifies good news of elderly people but danger to the young.

Pins.—Squabbles.

Play.—It is more fortunate to watch a Play than to dream that you are taking part in one.

Plough.—To dream of a Plough is good for marriage, courtship and such-like affairs ; but it requires some time to bring them to perfection. (Anc.)

Plums.—It is a good dream if you are gathering ripe Plums, but if they are still green, then your efforts will fail from want of careful planning. If you pick up the fruit after it has fallen to the ground, it is a sign of change of position, not entirely for your good. Dried Plums—such as Prunes—show difficulties.

Poison.—To dream that you have taken Poison is a warning of financial loss through some person whom you trust. Be careful how you give credit or lend money. Do not speculate or buy stocks or shares. If you recover from the effects of the Poison, you will get over your difficulties if you use care and tact.

Police.—This might be called a dream of contrary, for if you dream of trouble with the Police, it shows that some present difficulty will be overcome.

Pomegranate.—A happy augury ; honours will come to you.

Porcupine.—This unusual creature indicates difficulties in business.

Porter.—Slander and annoyance.

Postman.—Some unexpected happening.

Post Office.—A change of residence and companions.

Potatoes.—Do not try to play Providence for others or you may do more harm than good.

Pots.—A sign of coming disappointment. Be careful about your plans and do not talk them over with anyone.

Precipices.—To dream that one sees great and deep Precipices and that one falls over them, signifies that he that dreams will suffer much injury and hazard to his person and his goods be in danger by fire. (Anc.)

Priest.—To dream of a clergyman is a sign that some quarrel will be cleared up, thus increasing your personal happiness.

Prison.—This is a dream of contrary. It indicates much happiness in your home affairs and success in business.

Prize.—This is a contrary dream, foreboding loss through sharp dealing. Be on your guard when offered something cheap.

Procession.—To witness a Procession in your dream is a good sign to lovers, especially if the Procession be a long one.

Property.—(to see) this means you will be disappointed in your hopes.

Provisions.—It is a fortunate dream to see food on the table or provisions stored in the country.

Public House.—To dream of drinking in a Public House is a bad sign, to lovers it means deceit and to farmers failure.

Pudding.—A simple meal is a good omen in a dream.

Pump.—To pump clear water is a good sign, your business will prosper ; dirty water, however, signifies evil speaking.

Purse.—To dream of finding a purse containing money is a sign of success in love but not in business.

Puzzle.—An obstacle dream ; if you solve the puzzle your obstacles will be removed.

Q

Quails.—This is an unlucky dream, denoting bad intelligence and family jars. You will lose your lover through false reports.

Quarrels.—This is one of the dreams of contrary and fore-tells prosperity in your business affairs and re-union with friends.

Queen.—To dream that you see the King or Queen signifies honour, joy and much prosperity. (Anc.)

Questions.—To dream that someone is asking you questions is an obstacle omen. If you can answer properly, all will go well.

Quicksands.—This dream denotes that you are surrounded by many temptations. Do not be imprudent.

Quicksilver.—You will be invited to an enjoyable festivity. Gossip is on foot concerning you.

Quilt.—This is a fortunate dream, provided it is properly placed on the bed.

Quiver.—Happiness through the joys of home and marriage.

Quoits.—To a woman, it denotes some disagreeable and laborious undertaking to be gone through. To a man it is a sign of quarrelling.

R

Rabbit.—(Warren) costly enjoyment ; (to see Rabbits) increase of family.

Race.—To dream of running a Race is good to all, except they be sick persons when they dream they come to the end of their Race, for it signifies that shortly they shall come to the end of their life. (Anc.)

Rags.—This is a fortunate dream. Any display in a dream is generally a bad sign.

Rain.—A legacy or a present.

Rainbow.—Estrangement. (Anc.)

Ram.—Misfortune.

Rats.—Enemies ; (white) triumph over enemies.

Raven.—A bad omen ; (flying) news of a death ; (croaking) sadness.

Reading.—Your project is a dangerous one ; give it up.

Reaper.—The simple life for you.

Reptiles.—A subtle enemy.

Ribbons.—Pleasure and gaiety and foolish expenditure.

Rice.—To dream of eating Rice denotes abundance of instruction. (Anc.)

Riches.—Unfortunately this is a dream of contrary—the more flourishing your affairs in your visionary world, the worse they will be in real life.

Riddle.—An unexpected offer from someone related to you. Be on your guard as there is danger in it.

Riding.—It is a fortunate omen to dream that you are Riding a horse, unless the animal is out of control or throws you.

Ring.—Approaching wedding.

Rings.—The consummation of love.

Rival.—Domestic affliction and sorrow.

River.—(To fall in) envious enemies ; (to jump in) business disturbances and family troubles.

Road.—A well-made, broad Road is a most fortunate omen, but lanes or narrow winding paths should be treated as obstacles.

Roast Meat.—Affectionate greetings.

Robber or Thief.—It is considered fortunate to be molested by a Thief in your dream, provided you escape injury.

Robin.—One of Nature's most fortunate omens.

Rock.—Annoyance ; (to surmount) overcoming dangers.

Rocket.—Short-lived success is portended. You must build on firmer foundations next time.

Room.—(Strange) you will accomplish your designs.

Ropes.—These are obstacle dreams. If you find yourself securely bound with Ropes, then expect a difficult time in your business affairs, for trouble is surely coming.

Rosary.—To dream that you are telling the beads of your own Rosary means reconciliation with a friend ; to see someone wearing a Rosary signifies bereavement.

Roses.—Always good ; (full blown) good fortune and happiness ; (faded) success with a spice of danger.

Rowing.—It is a good omen if you dream of Rowing in a small boat. If others are Rowing with you, then expect to face difficulties before success. It is a bad sign if you lose or break an oar.

Rue.—Domestic difficulties.

Ruins.—It is a fortunate omen to dream that you are wandering amid the Ruins of some fine old building. If it is merely a modern house that has tumbled down, that is a bad sign. Beware of speculation.

Running.—This is generally an obstacle dream. If you succeed in reaching your goal, then all will go well.

Rust.—This being a sign of neglect is a bad omen and signifies loss through your own carelessness.

Rustling.—To dream of hearing the Rustling of wings is one of the best omens and means that your future will be protected and happy.

Rye.—Eating Rye bread in a dream is an excellent sign of success, especially in matters of love.

S

Sable.—The colour betokens tidings of loss ; the fur is a warning against extravagance. (Anc.)

Sack.—An obstacle. If the Sack is full and you empty it, then all will go well. But an empty Sack shows some difficulty that will probably cause loss.

Sacrifice.—A sign of coming festivities.

Saddle.—To dream that you are riding a horse without a Saddle, foretells ill-health through your own carelessness. Revise your plans at once and guard against mistakes. (Anc.)

Salad.—Your own qualities will ensure your advancement in the world.

Salmon.—Family trouble.

Salt.—This is a fortunate dream in every way, but if you spill the salt you may expect some difficulty and hard work before you succeed.

Sand.—Many small vexations.

Sapphire.—This is considered a fortunate dream, but it concerns your friends more than yourself.

Sash.—To dream of wearing one, a happy marriage.

Satin or Silk.—A fortunate dream for the business man, but the lover should beware of false and flattering words.

Saucepan.—See *Pots*.

Sausage.—Domestic troubles, often through ill-health.

Scissors.—A warning of false friends. Beware of giving your confidence too fully.

Sea.—A long but prosperous voyage.

Seals.—Uncertainty as to the results of a legal matter will vex you, but only for a short time.

Seat.—To dream that one has fallen from his Seat signifies that he shall be displaced from office.

Sermon.—Approaching indisposition.

Servant.—For a woman to dream that she is a Servant is an obstacle dream. Persevere and stick close to your job. To dream that you employ several Servants is an unfortunate omen.

Sew.—An obstacle dream. If your Sewing is successful and you complete the garment or other article, all will be well. But if you leave off before finishing the work, then look out for troubles.

Shawl.—Deep affection from one you love.

Sheep.—A fortunate dream, for it tells of coming success through well-conceived plans.

Shepherd.—This is considered a bad omen if you see no sheep at the time. If the flock is there also, then the presence of the Shepherd increases your difficulties, but will not stop your ultimate success.

Ship.—To dream that you are travelling in a Ship shows good fortune if you reach your destination safely.

Shipwreck.—A certain omen of disaster.

Shoes.—When patched, a sign of difficulties, but with hard work you will succeed. New Shoes show some fortunate enterprise with unexpected results.

Silver.—If one dreams he gathers up Silver, it signifies damage and loss. To see Silver eaten signifies great advantage. To eat Silver signifies wrath and anger. (Anc.)

Singing.—This is a dream of contrary, for it foretells troubles to come, but they will soon pass.

Skeleton.—To dream that you see a Skeleton is a sign of domestic trouble.

Sky.—Happiness ; (clouds) misfortune approaching ; (clear) serene life.

Smoke.—Some present success, but you will not really benefit by it. The denser the Smoke, the greater will be your disappointment.

Snails.—Intemperance and inconstancy.

Snakes.—This dream is a warning of treachery where you least expect it ; some unfortunate turn of events that you have not anticipated. Your plans will be wrecked.

Snow.—This is a very good dream, but you may have to work hard, especially if you find yourself walking in a Snow-storm.

Soldiers.—Loss of employment and probably many changes before you settle down once more.

Soles.—Misfortune and vexation.

Spade.—A new vista of contentment will open before you. Keep to beaten tracks when out alone.

Sparrow-Hawk.—Beware of your enemies.

Sparrows.—These friendly little birds denote hard work but with some success at the end.

Spider.—Good fortune ; (to kill one) enjoyment ; (spinning) money to come.

Stable.—A good companion will be yours for life.

Stag.—To see these noble animals is a good omen, but you must not molest or chase them, or you will ruin your own plans by your greed.

Stars.—(shooting) death of a relative.

Storks.—A promise of ill tidings.

Storm.—Dangers and difficulties.

Stranger.—News of a lost friend.

Straw.—Misfortune and losses.

Strawberries.—Unhoped-for success.

Sun.—(Rising) profits ; (setting) losses ; (clouded) bad news ; (bright) good news.

Supper.—News of a birth.

Swallow.—Successful enterprise ; (nest) happiness ; to) enter the house) constant friends.

Swans.—A good omen ; riches.

Swimming.—Hard work confronts you, but if you Swim to shore or reach your objective, then you will succeed in the end. (Mod.) Social Distinction. (Anc.)

Swing.—To dream of swinging is a sign of changing plans which will prove very successful.

Swoon.—To dream that you see a person swoon signifieth misfortune to a maid (Ancient meaning). To the married this is a sign of coming prosperity.

Swords.—All sharp-edged weapons or tools indicate bad news.

T

Table.—It is not fortunate to be seated at a Table in your dream ; but it is favourable if you see others thus seated.

Taffeta.—Wealth that will bring no satisfaction.

Tapestry.—Great enjoyment will come to you from small causes. (Mod.) Joy without adequate reason. (Anc.)

Tea.—Enjoyment.

Tears.—Joy and pleasure.

Theatre.—Sorrow caused by losses of money and of friends.

Thief or Thieves.—This is a bad dream if you are robbed and shows loss of money in any case.

Thimble.—Your occupation will be bettered.

Thirst.—If you appease it with good water, the omen is good ; if otherwise, the reverse.

Thistles.—Quarrels which may be avoided.

Thorns.—Disappointments in store ; (to be hurt) money troubles.

Thread.—To wind Thread denotes wealth gained by thrifty ways ; to break it, hard times ; to unravel knotted Thread, a mystery solved.

Throat.—It is generally considered a good sign if you dream of any trouble with your Throat.

Throne.—You will lose valuable friends in order to gain public distinction.

Thumb.—This is a dream of obstacles in your path. If any injury to your Thumb prevents you from using your hand, then expect business losses.

Thunder.—A Thunder Storm is a sign of great difficulties in store for you. Like all obstacle dreams, it depends upon what happens in your dream.

Tiger.—If you escape, good ; but beware of great danger if caught.

Till.—To dream of a shop Till filled with coins betokens a wealthy trader for a husband or a well dowered woman for a wife ; an empty Till is a warning of dishonest servants.

Timber.—To fell Timber is a presage of a long engagement ending in a happy marriage, unless the Timber seems to be old and rotten, in which case the engagement will be broken.

Tin.—A dream signifying that counterfeit friendship will be taken for true. Test your friends before you trust them.

Tinker.—Do not meddle in a friend's affairs after you have dreamed of a Tinker, or you will do more harm than good.

Toads.—You will be subjected to annoyance, but emerge triumphant.

Tortoise or Turtle.—Long life and success.

Tower.—(Ascending one) reverses in fortune.

Travelling.—(Through forest) obstacles which you will overcome ; (over hills) good fortune in store, but not easily accomplished.

Trees.—(In leaf) good ; (destroyed by storm) family troubles ; (leafless) deceptions ; (cut down) losses ; (to climb) better fortune.

Trinkets.—Your loved one is vain and fickle. Do not wear your heart upon your sleeve.

Trout.—Your troubles will vanish.

Trumpet or Cornet.—It is considered fortunate to hear the call of Trumpets in your dreams.

Tunnel.—Another obstacle dream; if you do escape from the Tunnel all will go well.

Turkey.—Trouble with your friends and with your business customers and associates.

Turnips.—Disappointment and vexation.

Turtle-Doves.—Affection soon to be bestowed upon you.

Twine.—A quarrel with a friend over a trifling matter will cause you more than trifling sorrow.

Twist.—To dream of anything which turns and twists is a sign of indecision, but to dream of twisted thread is an omen of good fortune through industry.

Twitter.—To dream of the twittering of birds signifieth the good influences of friends. (Anc.)

U

Ugliness.—It is a fortunate omen to dream of an Ugly person.

Umbrella.—A fortunate dream if you are carrying it open.

Unhappy.—A dream of contrary. The more miserable you are in your dream, the better for you in real life.

Unfortunate.—(Being so). Care will bring success.

Unicorn.—To dream of a fabulous creature presages anxiety caused by falsehoods.

Uniform.—This dream signifies a chance of promotion which will bring you the utmost good fortune in love as well as a better position.

Union Jack.—This is an excellent dream, denoting a chance to go abroad with a faithful marriage partner.

University.—A sign that you are fortunate in your talents and in your friends.

Unkind.—To dream of the Unkindness of one you love means the reverse. Your affection is as deeply returned.

Unlock.—A discovery will be made in your home ; do not try to keep a secret from those who love you.

Unmarried.—For married people to dream of being single again is a sign of danger from jealousy and gossip.

Uproar.—To dream of scenes of confusion and Uproar signifies an important decision which you will soon have to make.

Urn.—This portends news of very young relations who will cause you pride and delight in their achievements.

V

Vaccination.—You are in danger of giving more affection than its recipient is worth.

Valentine.—To dream you receive one predicts news of an old admirer who thinks of you still.

Valley.—Sickness of a temporary nature.

Vaults.—To dream of being in hollow cellars or deep Vaults signifies ill luck to new ventures for all except widows, to whom it means a second marriage. (Anc.)

Veal.—Certain good fortune.

Vegetables.—Hard work for little result will surely follow a dream of these Green offerings of Nature. Persevere and do not lose heart.

Veil.—To dream that you are wearing a Veil is a bad sign, even if it is a Bridal Veil, unless you remove it before the dream is concluded.

Velvet.—A fortunate dream, but it will depend largely upon the colour. See *Colour*.

Vermin.—Nearly all unpleasant dreams of this sort go by " contraries " and mean good luck.

Villa.—To dream that you are going over a fine Villa is a sign that you will be very happy in a small one before long.

Village.—This dream promises an offer of a change which will prove most important to your future.

Villain.—To dream of a Ruffian or a Villain denotes a letter or present from one you love.

Vinegar.—Useless toil. (Mod.) Signifies sickness through drink. (Anc.)

Vintage.—Successful business operations and affection rewarded.

Violets.—Success in enterprise ; (out of season) newly awakened affection.

Vision.—Danger to the person who appears to you.

Visit.—To pay a Visit, obstacles to your plans ; to receive a Visit from a friend signifies travel for pleasure.

Visitors.—It is not a good omen to dream of Visitors ; the more people there are around you, the greater will be your business difficulties.

Voice.—To hear people speaking is a dream of contrary. If they appear to be happy and merry, then expect reverses in business and many worries.

Volcano.—To dream of a Volcano, foretells great disagreements, family jars and lovers' quarrels. To a man of commerce it portends dishonest servants and a robbery or some sad convulsion. To lovers it is a design on one side.

Voyage.—A message from a distance is soon to be received.

Vulture.—Dangerous enemies ; (to kill) conquest of misfortune ; (to see one devouring its prey) your troubles will cease and fortune smile upon you.

W

Wading.—It is considered a good sign for lovers if they dream of Wading in clear water. If the water is muddy or rough disillusion will soon come.

Wafted.—To dream of being Wafted along without walking is a sign of small vexations.

Wager.—This portends losses ; act cautiously.

Wages.—To receive them, danger of small thefts ; to pay them, money from a legacy.

Wagon.—To dream that you are driving in a Wagon is a sign of loss of money ; but if a loaded wagon or cart comes to your door then some unexpected good fortune will come to you.

Walls.—Dangerous enterprises, unless you climb over them easily, when they betoken business success.

Walnuts.—All nuts show small difficulties that need not prove serious if attacked earnestly. (Mod.) Troubles (Anc.)

Warehouse.—A dream of good omen. You will be successful in business and in married life.

Warts.—To see Warts on your hand in a dream indicates as many sums of money as you can see Warts to come to you ; on the hands of others means rich friends.

Washing.—A dream of difficulties ahead, probably connected with friends or in your home life.

Wasps.—Enemies amongst those whom you trust. (Mod.) Vexation. (Anc.)

Watch.—A journey by land.

Watchman.—You are protected by silent love and friendship near you.

Water.—(Drinking) a bad omen ; (to fall into) reconciliation ; (bathing) misfortune and disappointments.

Water-Carrier.—Money increases.

Water-Cress.—Danger in love affairs, especially if you gather it.

Water-Lilies.—Your wish is out of reach ; do not try to gain it, lest further loss ensue.

Water-Mill.—To dream of being in a Water-Mill is a favourable omen. To a tradesman it denotes increase of business ; to the farmer, abundant crops ; in love, success and happiness.

Waves.—You must be prepared to fight for fortune.

Wayfarer.—To dream of meeting a Wayfarer on a lonely path is a sign of a new friend.

Wax.—Neither borrow nor lend money in the near future or you will regret it.

Weeding.—Happiness and good fortune.

Weeping.—To dream one Weeps is a sign of joy and mirth to come.

Well.—(To draw water, success and profit). To fall in signifies an almost unavoidable danger.

Wheat.—Riches will be yours.

Whirlwind.—Dangerous reports.

Widow.—To dream that you converse with a Widow foreshadows loss of someone dear to you either by death or unfaithfulness.

Wig.—A proposal soon to come, if the dreamer be an unmarried woman ; for a man to dream of a Wig signifies a secret love-affair.

Wilderness.—A festive occasion in your home is soon to lead you to new interests.

Will.—Dreaming of making your Will signifies improved health and fortunes.

Willow.—Do not trust a new acquaintance ; good news of an old friend.

Wind.—Good news is coming ; the stronger the gale of Wind the sooner you may expect good fortune.

Windmill.—Some gain, but only of a small character.

Wine.—A sign of a comfortable home life ; it does not refer to business or love affairs.

Wings.—A bad omen ; you will lose money.

Winter.—To dream of a wintry scene with snow on the ground is an omen of prosperity, but to dream of Summer in Winter is the reverse.

Wireless.—Unexpected good news about money.

Wishing Well.—Two lovers to choose from. Think well before deciding.

Witch.—An ill omen in every way.

Witness.—To dream of being a Witness in court is a warning to be on your guard against false accusations which will be made against you.

Wizard.—Family prosperity and contentment.

Wolf.—Enmity ; (To kill one) success ; (To pursue) dangers overcome ; (Pursued by) danger and anxiety.

Wood-Cutter.—Your efforts will not result in much profit.

Workhouse.—A legacy to come before long.

Workman.—Your enterprise will meet its reward.

Workshop.—A sign of good fortune.

Worms.—Danger of infectious disease.

Wreck.—Threatened trouble to health or business.

Wrestling.—An unfortunate dream denoting losses through ill-health. (Mod.) Sorrow and sickness. (Anc.)

Write.—To dream one Writes on paper signifies accusations to be made against you. (Anc.)

Writing.—Good news from an unexpected quarter. (Mod.)

Y

Yacht.—To see one means good luck if the sea be smooth ;

to be in one, ambitions realised, unless the sea be rough, which means disappointment.

Yarn.—You will receive a fine present from an unexpected quarter.

Yawning.—An obstacle dream, but not of serious import.

Yeast.—Money which has been accumulated by thrift will be left to you under strange conditions.

Yell.—To dream of hideous Yells and noises is a sign of peace after strife.

Yew-Tree.—This dream denotes the death of an aged person from whom you will receive a legacy which will place you above want. If you sit under a Yew-Tree, it foretells that your life will not be long ; but if you merely gaze upon it you will have many years of happy life.

Yoke.—You are too much under the influence of an older person. Try to develop your own personality.

Young.—To dream that you have become young again is a favourable omen.

Z

Zebra.—Disagreement with friends.

Zeppelin.—A dream signifying ambition far beyond your reach.

Zoological Gardens.—Although wild animals in captivity are not generally good signs when seen singly it is considered a favourable omen to visit a collection of them in cages.

SECTION IV

OMENS—ANCIENT AND MODERN

IN remote ages, as far back as the Babylonian and Assyrian civilisations, not only were dreams studied, but omens were regarded as of very great importance. Indeed, all over the world, even the uncivilised races developed a belief in omens, and made a collection of them almost as soon as they developed a language of their own. In India, and in Greece also, where the records and traditions of the early ages of civilisation have been handed down from the dim past, omens have always been considered of great significance.

That there is good ground for belief in some omens, seems indisputable ; though whether this has arisen as the result of experience, by the happening of some particular event close upon the heels of signs observed ; or whether it has been an intuitive science in which premonition has been used to affect an interpretation, is not quite clear. It seems idle to attempt to dismiss the whole subject as one of mere superstition, guessing, or abject credulity, as some people try to do ; the fact remains, that omens in numerous cases have been found to give useful warnings. To say that these are just mere coincidences, is to beg the question, for the universe is governed by laws set and fixed as the universe itself. There is no such thing as accident or coincidence in these laws, they conform to fixed rules. We may not be able to see the steps or recognise the connections, but that does not mean that they are not existent.

Written on tablets by the Babylonian and Assyrian priests, and which have been preserved in the British Museum, events were predicted which they believed would happen in the near and remote future. The priests deduced these omens from the appearance and actions of animals, birds, fish and reptiles ; from the appearance of the entrails of sacrificial victims ; from the appearance and conditions of human and animal offspring at birth ; from the state and condition of various members of the human body.

Other signs were deduced from the symptoms of sick men ; from the events or actions of a man's life ; from dreams and visions ; from the appearance of a man's shadow ; from fire-light or smoke ; from the state and condition of cities and their streets, or fields, marshes, rivers and lands. From the appearance of the stars and planets, of eclipses, meteors, or shooting stars, the direction of the wind, the form of clouds, from thunder and lightning and other weather incidents, they were able to forecast happenings. A whole host of tablets are devoted to these predictions.

It is possible that many of these omens found their way into Greece. It is not unreasonable to believe that India may have derived her knowledge of omens from Babylonia ; or indeed that it may have been the other way about. The greatest scholars to-day, are divided in their opinions as to which was the earlier civilisation.

But the point to be made here, is that in all parts of the world—in quarters where we may be certain that no trace of Grecian, Hindoo, or Babylonian science or civilisation has appeared—there are still to be found various systems of predictions by means of omens.

This may be accounted for in two ways. One, that all races as they grow up, develop the same course of evolution of ideas and superstitions which to many may appear childish. The other explanation seems to be the more reasonable one, if we believe, as we seem bound to do, that omens do foretell—that all peoples, all races, accumulate a record, oral or written, of events that happened more or less in connection with signs which seemed to indicate them. In course of time this knowledge seems to consolidate. It becomes firmly fixed in mind and generally accepted as true ; then it is handed down from one generation to another, and often, with the passage of time, it becomes distorted and twisted from its original meaning.

It would be difficult to attempt to classify omens, but mainly they may be divided into two divisions ; omens of good luck, and omens of bad fortune.

Naturally, as these omens may be said to have originated in the childhood of civilisations, many of the meanings must seem childish and primitive. The body enters primarily into the meanings of omens. With most races, the right-hand side indicated good, the left-hand bad.

If the palms of the hands itched, then a near handling of money was foreshadowed. The right hand would receive money, the left would be used to pay out. If the ears tingled or burned, someone was talking of the person ; good for the right ear, bad for the left. In Greece, a sneeze was a good omen ; it was considered a proof of veracity of what was said at the moment by the one who sneezed. Moles, with which we deal later in this section, also entered largely into the question of omens.

Next to the human body itself, came the animals and birds and the various objects of nature, and Greece as well as Egypt paid especial attention to omens and their divination by the observance of birds. In Greece, some of the gods and goddesses were believed to have taken the shape of birds and animals, and birds especially were held sacred.

The raven was considered the bird of death, due probably to its sable hue, not only in Grecian mythology ; in Norse as well we have the ravens of Odin as signs of death.

The peacock is considered a bird of ill luck. In Grecian mythology the giant Argus was set by jealous Juno to watch the maid Io, beloved of her spouse Jupiter. To save Io, Jupiter changed her into a heifer, and sent Hermes to kill Argus while he was asleep. Juno had the giant's eyes shown in the tail of her favourite bird in memory of her servant.

A bird (though a human in bird form) warned Ulysses against the wiles of the sorceress Circe.

Of the animals, the wolf was sacred to Apollo, the Sun God, the dragon and panther to Bacchus the God of wine, the Stag to Diana, the goddess of the hunt ; the serpent to Aesculapius ; to Jupiter, the Eagle ; to Juno, the peacock and the lamb ; to Mars the God of war, the horse ; to Neptune God of the Sea, the Bull ; and to Vulcan, god of fire and the forge, the lion.

In other countries, too, both birds and animals were held sacred. In Egypt the Hawk was held sacred because it was the form assumed by the God Horus, and the Ibis because it was said that the god Thoth escaped in the form of this bird from the pursuit of Typhon. To kill one, therefore, was visited with death.

In Sweden, the stork is held sacred on account of the legend that it flew round the Cross, when Jesus was crucified, crying " Styrka, Styrka." It is the sworn foe of snakes, and held in veneration.

In Cornwall, choughs are still protected, because in legendary lore the soul of King Arthur was changed into the body of a chough.

The stormy petrels of the sea are called Mother Carey's Chickens, because sailors believed that this mythical person took the souls of sailors drowned at sea and put them in her birds.

Swans are protected in Ireland because of a legend of a maiden being transformed into a swan.

All these birds therefore have been watched, and their movements in daily life as well as in dreams have been used as omens by the people around them. W. H. Halliday in his book on Greek Divination, gave many curious instances of bird omens which were fulfilled, as also the Rev. F. G. Lee in his book, *The Other World*.

In the ancient family of Ferrers of Chartley Park in Staffordshire, a herd of wild cattle is preserved. A tradition arose in the reign of Henry III, that the birth of a parti-coloured calf was a sure sign of death, within the same year, to a member of Lord Ferrer's family. This came true, and whether by coincidence or not, it is recorded that whenever a calf of this description has been born, a death has followed in the family.

Another ancient book, *Divination by Birds and Beasts*, says : " It hath been observed by the learned in all ages that our all wise and beneficent Creator originally implanted in the frame of Nature a means whereby mankind may attain to the knowledge of such future contingencies as may concern their future happiness ; and especially since we observe that even the most inconsiderable creatures are more or less endowed with a gift of foreknowledge."

After a dissertation upon the great sagacity with which the various creatures are endowed, the writer goes on to say, " Observe when you go out of your house to do any kind of business ; if on the way, you see a man or a bird, going or flying, so that either of them set themselves before you on your right hand, that is a good sign for your business. But when you see a bird or man before you on your left side, it is an ill omen. When either a man or a bird overtake you, coming from the right side of you and turning towards the left, then going from your sight, that is a sign of good fortune.

" Should you observe a man or a bird moving, which then rests before you on your right side, and then see him or it move on again, you have watched an omen of success in your business.

" Should you observe a man or a bird approaching you and turning from your right side to your left, then it is an ill omen for your business. But when either of them overtake you from behind, and move faster than you, but before overtaking you they come to a halt on your right side, it is a good omen, but if on your left side, it is a bad sign.

" A man or a bird coming from your left side to the right, and going right out of sight without halting, signifies good fortune. A man or bird coming from your right side behind you to the left and then halting, is an ill omen.

" The signs which occur at the beginning of any undertaking must also be observed. For instance, if about to start new work or enter on a fresh proposition, if it is found that mice have gnawed your clothes or your papers, then leave the business alone, for it will not prosper. If on setting forth from your house, you chance to stumble upon the threshold, or on the way, then postpone your journey.

" If any ill omen should happen at the outset of your business, forbear the work for a while lest it prove a disappointment to you.

" Finally, do not turn back at the beginning of a journey, if something has been forgotten ; try to carry through without it, or postpone your appointment."

The Divination of Omens

Naturally, the growth of the number of omens depended upon observation, but many diviners went a step further and obtained omens by the action of substances. These were dropped into a bowl of water, and the shapes which they took were interpreted according to the knowledge of the diviner. The substance varied in different countries; in some, water was used; while in various countries even to-day, melted lead, melted wax, or the white of an egg are used. From the shapes which result, the trade or fortune of a future husband may be shown, the coming luck of the year, and so on, are deduced as omens in the folk practices of modern Europe. The Finns use melted stearine, a kind of wax, and also melted lead; Magyars, lead; Russians, wax; Danes, lead and white of egg.

Some famous omens include that told to Loetychides II of Sparta. A viper became entangled in the handle of the city key, and the soothsayers said that his expedition would fail. " Not so " he replied. " The key got the viper, and I have killed it."

When Julius Cæsar landed at Adrumetum in Africa, he slipped and fell. This was considered a fatal omen, but with presence of mind, he exclaimed, " Thus do I take possession of thee, O Africa." The story was told of Scipio, and also of William the Conqueror, when he fell on the shore at Bulverhythe.

No fixed laws can be laid down as to the real truth of omens. If people are superstitious, and believe in the approach of trouble because of the omen, it often happens; but possibly more by coincidence than actually due to the omen.

A LIST OF OMENS AND THEIR MEANINGS

Ants.—Should these sagacious insects over-run a place where they have never been seen before, prosperous times will follow them, for they are an omen of industry. Where they have over-run a place and suddenly deserted it altogether, idleness and bad times will descend upon the dwellers therein.

Ass.—See *Mule.*

Bees.—Are weather-wise insects.' They hover near the hive and do not venture far away when storms are at hand.

Birds.—These are perhaps the most well-known and important fortune-tellers in the world of omens. The farmyard **cock** begins the list. Should he come to meet you, or several of them crowd round your house, visitors, successful journeys and business are signified; but should he crow when a newly-married couple come to the house, ill fortune awaits them. Crows croaking over a person are evil omens; so also are jackdaws and ravens. The magpie predicts news of company; good should it appear on the right hand, and bad if it come from the left; two magpies mean good luck, three a wedding, four a birth. The screech owl is an omen of theft and robbery, especially if it should nest in a building. Sparrows are fortunate to lovers but to no one else.

Birthdays.—The following is an old adage :—

> " Sunday's child is full of grace,
> Monday's child is fair of face,
> Tuesday's child is sorry and sad,
> Wednesday's child is merry and glad,
> Thursday's child has far to roam,
> Friday's child will stay at home ;
> But Saturday's child is fond of giving
> However hard he work for his living."

Another version, however, runs thus :—

> " Monday's child is fair of face,
> Tuesday's child is full of grace,
> Wednesday's child is full of woe,
> Thursday's child has far to go,
> Friday's child is loving and giving,
> Saturday's child must work for its living ;
> But the child that is born on the Sabbath Day
> Is handsome and wise and good and gay."

Candle.—A spark on the wick of a Candle indicates a letter coming to the one who sees it first ; while a big glow upon the wick foretells money coming to the one who lit the Candle. Candles burning with a blue flame indicate the presence of spirits.

Cats.—" Should a Cat cross the road in front of you, turn back and postpone your hourney," says an olden-time writer ; " but should a black cat come to meet you from the right-hand side, you are sure to succeed."

Clothes.—To put on Clothes inside out is an excellent omen, but they should not be turned right side out until it is time to take them off, or the luck will be changed. If it is necessary to alter them, ask another person to remove them so that you do not change them yourself.

Crickets. These should never be disturbed, for they foretell money coming to the house they inhabit.

Death-Watch Beetle.—A clicking in the wall by this little insect is regarded as evil, but it does not necessarily mean a death ; possibly only news of sickness.

Dog.—To meet a Dog first thing on setting out, indicates good fortune coming to you through a friend.

Donkey.—See *Mule.*

Ears.—If your Ears tingle, it is a sign that you are being talked about. Some say, " Right for spite, left for love." Others say, " Right for Mother, left for lover, or brother."

Eel.—To see an Eel, predicts that you will find work with a master hard to please.

Flies.—These are not very good signs, indicating that you will be met with impudence and importunity from your inferiors.

Fruit Stones or Pips.—Country maidens count their cherry-stones, and the letters of the alphabet till they come to the letter corresponding to the number of the stones. This indicates the initial of their sweetheart. Another omen is made by thinking of a wish, and then counting the stones or pips. If the number is even, the omen is a good one ; if odd, the reverse.

Gnats.—Flying high betokens fair weather on the morrow and also good fortune.

Goats.—To meet Goats when you are on the way to a new enterprise, is a sign of success through perseverance.

Grasshopper.—To see or hear this insect, foretells a lucky journey.

Hare.—This is an unlucky sign ; turn back from your projects if possible.

Hay.—To pass a cart loaded with Hay portends good fortune.

Hog or Pig.—This animal is a bad omen, and if met with on a journey, another day should be chosen. See *Pigs.*

Horses.—To see Horses drawing a conveyance is considered a good omen, especially if you overtake and pass them.

Horseshoe.—To find one, especially just as it is cast from the horse's foot, is considered one of the luckiest of all omens. It should be nailed on the front door, but right way up, the ends at the top so as to hold in the luck. If reversed, the luck drops out.

Knives.—If Knives become crossed, it is held to indicate bad luck or a coming quarrel If a knife, or fork, or the point of scissors falling to the ground, stick fast to the floor, a visitor is coming ; while if you wish before removing the instrument, your wish will be granted.

Ladybirds.—Betokens visitors.

Locusts.—Are a bad sign, especially if they stay long in one place.

Marriage.—A maid should not wear colours ; a widow, never white. Happy omens for brides are sunshine and a cat sneezing.

May.—" Marry in May and you'll rue the day."

Mice.—These timid creatures are, oddly enough, omens of a personal danger.

Mule or Ass.—This is an omen of trouble through foolishness ; not necessarily your own.

Nails.—" Cut them on Monday, cut for wealth,
        Cut them on Tuesday, cut for good health,
        Cut them on Wednesday, cut for a letter,
        Cut them on Thursday for something better,
        Cut them on Friday, cut for a wife,
        Cut them on Saturday, cut for long life,
        Cut them on Sunday, cut them for evil,
        For all the next week you'll be ruled by the devil."

New Moon.—On a Monday, signifies good luck and good weather. The New Moon seen for the first time over the right shoulder offers the chance for a wish to come true, but seen through glass, means that your wish will not come true. Turn your silver over when first observing the New Moon and it will increase before the month is out.

Nightingale.—Lucky for lovers if heard before the cuckoo.

Owls.—Continuous hooting of Owls in your trees is said to be an omen of ill-health.

Oxen.—These are good signs, especially when seen by people born in the month of April or May.

Pigs.—To meet a Sow coming towards you is good ; but if she turns away, the luck flies. See *Hog*.

Pips.—See *Fruit Stones*.

Rabbits.—A Rabbit running across your path is said to be unlucky.

Rats.—For Rats to leave a building where they have once nested, means disaster to those who live in it. If they gnaw your clothes, be cautious in undertaking any new or risky business.

Salt.—Spilled, means a quarrel or some ill luck. This may be avoided by throwing a pinch over the left shoulder.

Shoe or Boot Lace.—Should these persistently come untied, you will soon hear surprising news.

Shoes.—The right Shoe is the best one to put on first.

Shooting Stars.—If you wish while the star is still moving, your wish will come true.

Singing.—Before breakfast, you'll cry before night.

Snake.—If you meet with a Snake, beware of the tongue of an enemy. A viper on the path signifies a spiteful woman in your way.

Spiders.—The little Red Spider is the Money Spider, and means good fortune coming to you. It must not be disturbed. Long-legged Spiders are also forerunners of good fortune. The Spider weaving a line downwards signifies success to your undertakings. It is considered most unlucky to kill a spider, especially in the house.

Stones.—See *Fruit Stones.*

Straw.—To see a cart loaded with Straw is considered a sign of approaching bad fortune. Some people hold that it is the sign of a death.

Stumble.—To Stumble indicates coming trouble, but mainly obstacles in your path.

Trip.—To Trip over a mat or when going upstairs, signifies an approaching wedding at the house.

Washing Hands.—If you wash your hands in the water just used by another, a quarrel may be expected, unless you first make the sign of the cross over the water.

TRADITIONAL OMENS

Many observances have been made into omens, which to disobey is supposed to bring trouble.

For instance, for a bride, a maid should marry only in white, while a widow should always choose colours, but not green, black or yellow.

Brides should not choose the month of May, nor the thirteenth of the month.

If a flight of birds is seen on the way to church, it is an indication of a large family.

To meet a funeral on the way to a wedding is considered a bad sign; one of speedy separation, or at least many quarrels.

" Blessed is the bride that the sun shines on," has become a proverbial omen, and even on a dull day, if the sun emerges suddenly from behind a cloud, it is a good sign, while if it shines on the altar during the service, it denotes future prosperity and connubial bliss.

To pass under a ladder is unlucky.

To fail to wish when a pie-bald horse passes you is unlucky.

Never pick up an odd glove in the street Pass it by and leave the bad luck behind you.

If you drop your umbrella, let someone else pick it up, it is unlucky for you to do so yourself. It is also considered unlucky to open an umbrella inside the house.

Never tell a dream before breakfast, and never relate a Friday's dream if bad. The proverb runs, " Friday's dream on Saturday told, is sure to come true before nine days old."

A falling picture, or a howling dog, are well-known omens of death. The flight of one or more ravens over a house also betokens the approach of death.

To most people all these omens are considered as old-fashioned superstitions, yet many secretly believe in them though outwardly deriding them, and these people will often wear either openly or hidden in their clothes or bags, some mascot that they consider will avert the ill luck, or bring them good fortune.

A sprig of heather is lucky, but only to Scottish folk, for it is their native emblem.

A horse-shoe or wish-bone is often used in brooch form. Eastern folk use the five-pointed star ; western, take a lucky pig, or a black cat as luck signs.

Many people also prefer to conduct their business, especially when starting anything fresh, on their lucky or natal day of the week. Fridays and Tuesdays are the best general days for women ; Sundays and Mondays for men. There are three months of the year in which it is not considered lucky to sign a lease or enter into a new house, namely April, July and November. The eleventh of any month is also considered bad for such projects.

MOLES AS OMENS

Many people not content with seeing omens in objects and occurrences around them, regard moles on the human body as indications of the future, and omens of fortune or misfortune, according to circumstances. Shape, size and position are all regarded as omens. If round, oblong or angular, each shape alters the omen. The larger the mole, the greater is likely to be either good or bad fortune, the smaller, the reverse. A round mole is good ; oblong, but a moderate share of good fortune ; if angular, a mixture of good and bad luck. The deeper the colour, the more it indicates favour or disgrace, the lighter the colour, the less of either. A hairy mole indicates misfortune, one with a few long hairs, indicate good fortune.

The position alters the omen. A mole on the right side of the forehead or right temple signifies approaching wealth and honour.

A mole on the right eyebrow denotes a speedy and early marriage free from long engagements.

If on the left side, disappointments will be the fate.

Moles near the corner of either eyes, show a person of steady habit, but liable to a sudden death.

A mole on either cheek is believed to show one who will never achieve great fortune, but neither will they fall into poverty.

A mole on the nose is said to be lucky, though this seems unreasonable.

One on the chin, foretells prosperity and esteem.

A mole on the throat indicates that the person will become rich, not by his own endeavours, but through marriage.

A mole on the right breast denotes a sudden reverse from comfort to distress by accidents.

A mole on the left breast signifies success in undertakings, especially those of an amorous nature.

A mole on the bosom portends mediocrity of health and fortune.

A mole under the left breast over the heart signifies that a man will be of a warm disposition, but unsettled in habit. In a lady, sincerity in love.

A mole on the right side of the body denotes a person of slow understanding.

A mole on either hip promises a large family.

A mole on the right thigh indicates wealth and success in marriage.

A mole on the left thigh foreshadows much suffering from poverty and want of friends, as well as enmity and injustice from others.

A mole on the right knee indicates the choice of a good life partner and few disappointments.

A mole on the left knee portends that the person is apt to be rash, but honest and of good behaviour generally.

A mole on either leg shows that the person is inclined to be indolent and thoughtless.

To judge the fate of any one, first find out the characteristics of the time and date of birth, examine the features of the person, use the science of palmistry and physiognomy, and couple it with this prognostication by moles. See how they agree in respect to their several accounts and make judgment accordingly.

MASCOTS TO AVERT ILL OMENS

Though not perhaps, strictly speaking, coming within the scope of Omens themselves, yet many people taking no risks as to probability or truth of ill omens, may yet like to learn of special mascots which have been supposed to hold means of averting ill fortune.

The ancients had a mystic word, " Abracadabra," which they inscribed on a slip of parchment and fastened it around their necks. Thus worn, the person was supposed to be protected against evil spirits, but it had to be written in the form of a triangle thus.

ABRACADABRA
BRACADABR
RACADAB
ACADA
CAD
A

It will be noticed that the word can be read along the top line and also down and up the two sides of the triangle.

Since the days of the Norman Conquest, it was considered lucky to carry a dried acorn.

People who lived near the sea regard the anchor as a symbol of hope, safety and good fortune, and if worn, might save the loved one from drowning.

Arrowheads have served as charms since the earliest times. These in primitive days were made of flint and small enough to be suspended round the neck. They were supposed to ward off the evil eye.

The ancients carved suitable pieces of stone to the shape of axe-heads, and used them the same as arrowheads.

A very old talisman, only seen in ancient documents, consists of a ring, the rim of which is filled with triangles. Stretched across the ring is a stick which shows seven knots, like a piece of bamboo, and across this lies a serpent. The ring stands for eternity, which like the ring has neither beginning nor end. The triangles within the rim symbolise the three of the Trinity. The seven knots stand for the seven degrees of learning, while the serpent was the sign of wisdom.

Almost as old as the ring, the bangle is a symbol that the wearer has become the " slave " or the loved possession of the giver of the ornament.

Beads have formed the ornaments as well as mascots of all nations, from the coloured beads of the Indians, to the amber and pearl necklaces of the western world. Beads were supposed to protect children from the Evil Eye, and the special charm of childhood is coral.

Bees made into mascots are supposed to give the wearers remarkable powers of endurance, perseverance and commercial ability. They are considered specially potent in working for the good of those who deal in merchandise, or are connected with buying and selling.

Bells too were supposed to have the power of frightening away the evil spirits ; thus people carried small bells about them in order to be proof against evil. The tolling of a church bell is a custom which grew out of that belief.

Black cats were the witches' pet, and akin to the proverb, " Love me, love my dog." People perhaps went out of their way to treat black cats kindly, lest they brought down on them the wrath of the witch, hence " black cats are lucky."

The Bull mascot is simply an emblem of strength.

Clover is lucky if it has four leaves.

A poem says :—

" One leaf for fame
And one for wealth
A third for a faithful lover,
Yet another to bring you glorious health
And all in a four-leaf clover."

Coal is lucky if you find a piece, but not if bought in the ordinary way of household purchases. A whole year of good luck is bestowed on the household if a dark man carrying a piece of coal is the first person to cross the threshold after the Old Year has gone out.

The Cornucopia or Horn of Plenty, dates from the horns of mead and ale drunk at harvest festivals. The idea is that the horns are symbolical of plenty.

The symbol of the fish has also always been regarded as a sign of increase and plenty, and it is often seen cut out of mother-of-pearl, the inner shell of the oyster, and used as a charm. In ancient days it represented Dagon, the Sun Fish, and was worshipped by the Syrians. The fish symbol is not given only to the talismanic art of the Philistines, it enters into the rites of the Hebrews, though they may have adopted it during their captivity in the cities. The name Dag is Hebrew for Fish, and as Dagon it is suggested that the Sun was worshipped on its entry into the Sign of the Fishes—Pisces.

A favourite charm also is the Hand. It is supposed to represent the Hand of Fatima, the daughter of Mahomet. The fingers stand for the qualities, Hospitality, Generosity, Strength and Goodness, the thumb for power, and it was supposed that anyone wearing this charm would gain these virtues.

The Horsehoe has always been the symbol of luck. The legend runs that the Devil asked St. Dunstan, whose hobby was shoeing horses, to shoe his " single hoof." The Saint recognised his customer, and tied him tightly to the wall. Then he proceeded with his task, but gave the devil such pain, that he roared for mercy. St. Dunstan released him only on condition that the devil would never enter a place where he saw the horse-shoe nailed on the door. So prevalent is the belief in the luck of this mascot that Lord Nelson even had one nailed to the mast of his ship the *Victory*.

The Greek Key figures in many patterns, and may be termed a mascot for it symbolised life. Another form consists of three keys intertwined. One stood for love, a second for wealth and the third for health. The keys were supposed to unlock the doors which led to these desirable qualities.

A knot stands for the joining of two things, hence we have lucky sailors' knots, and the " true lovers' knots."

The Shamrock dates from the time of the Druids, who termed it a harbinger of good luck, and the Irish have adopted it as their national emblem.

Although the fashion for the Swastika has dropped down to zero, yet it is not of German origin, but of Sanscrit birth, and means " purveyor of good fortune." It is meant to affirm that we reap what we sow, and that present effects are the result of past happenings.

Each person should wear the particular charm and particularly the jewel of his birth month. For this reason is appended a guide to the special Sign of the Zodiac beneath which people are born, with their proper birth stone to act as a mascot against ill fortune.

The Zodiac is an imaginary belt in the sky through which the Heavenly bodies were supposed to trace regular paths. The ancient astrologers divided this belt into twelve portions, giving to each the especial name and sign. Long years of study enabled the astrologers to note the influences of the Sun when it entered these Zodiacal divisions, and these influences are brought to bear upon the characteristics and life chances of the individuals whose birth months are in the various Zodiacal divisions. The twelve months of the Zodiac, however, do not correspond with the modern calendar. The Zodiacal periods commence on the 19th to the 22nd of the month, and terminate on a similar date in the following month. Thus Capricorn, which rules the period between December 22nd and January 20th, would be the Sign of people born within those dates, but for others who were born later in January, their real Zodiacal Sign would be February, and they might partake of the qualities and characteristics of the two months. To such folk, the mascots of either or both months may be used. It is held to be lucky to use the personal Zodiacal Sign, whether in the form of ornament or seal. Below is given just the mascots of the month as it falls between its right dates.

January Mascots

Those whose birthday falls in the first month of the year are born for power, and should wear garnets in preference to all other gems, in order to avert ill omens and evil influences ; for the garnet is under the planetary influence of Saturn, the powerful planet. This stone ensures to its wearer true friendship and faithfulness. In olden days, knights whose ladies were January born, gave them jewels of garnet, in the belief that the power of these gems would ensure their fidelity while they were absent from one another. The same planet rules the jet and all black stones. For this reason all Capricorn people derive good luck from the colours, black, dark brown and red. Their lucky day of the week is Saturday. The Zodiacal Sign is Aquarius, the Water Carrier.

February Mascots

Those who are born in this month come under Pisces, the Fish, and can ensure peace of mind by wearing the Amethyst. Mars and Jupiter are their protective planets, who rule the crystal, moonstone and jasper. All shades of blue are lucky to them.

March Mascots

Born under the Sign of Aries the Ram, March-born folk are protected by Mars, and all colours of scarlet are lucky for them. Strength is given them for they are destined to meet with many dangers and should wear the blood-stone to ensure courage and success in overcoming them. This unusual looking gem is a kind of jasper or quartz, crystallised with gold, from which it derives its glint of depth and colour. Lovers who are born in this month are invariably successful if they wear this stone, and it is also supposed to guard the health of the March-born wearers. Mars is their protective planet, jasper their secondary jewel and Aries, the Ram, their astrological sign.

April Mascots

No more beautiful stone for an amulet could be imagined than that dedicated to the April born, for the month stone is the diamond, emblem of innocence and averter of all omens of evil. The Sun is the protective planet and Chrysolite their secondary stone.

The diamond used to be considered a safe-guard against plagues, evil spirits and poisons of mind or body, endowing its wearer with success in love and war. It should be worn upon the left arm so that it can touch the skin. Taurus, the Bull, is the Zodiacal sign.

May Mascots

Legend has it, that should a person born in May and wearing the emerald, which is the month's mascot, encounter an evil influence so strong that the protective jewel is not powerful enough to overcome it, the mascot will warn its owner by crumbling into fragments or falling from its setting. It is supposed to guard those born in May from fevers, loss of sight and memory. Venus, Jupiter and Mercury are all influential planets under whose rule the emerald comes, and the Moon too is favourably inclined, so that May born subjects should be well protected. Green jasper, beryl and alabaster are their secondary stones, and Gemini, the Twins, their astrological sign.

June Mascots

The agate preserves the health and wealth of the wearer whose birthday falls in June. The Ancients believed it to possess the property of soothing pain or an agitated mind, preserving the wearer from the bites of snakes or scorpions and averting accidents. Their colours vary from milk-white and yellow, to blue, brick-red, brown, violet and even black, and frequently the forms of trees, animals and even figures are seen within the stone. Zircon and coral are the secondary stones of the month, presided over by Venus, the planet of beauty and peace, of which all June-born people inherit a share. Cancer, the Crab, is the astrological sign.

July Mascots

Those born in Midsummer are fortunate in claiming the ruby as their month stone. This endows them with wisdom, sympathy and freedom from care, as might be expected. The sun is their guardian, white topaz and chrysolite their secondary birth stones, and Leo, the Lion, their Zodiacal sign.

August Mascots

Those who are born in August and do not wear a sardonyx, must, it is said, " live unloved and alone." This composite stone, uniting in itself the nature and colours of the onyx and red cornelian, which vary from bright red to milky-white, or even pale green where an admixture of chalcedony is found in the stone. Venus is the ruling planet, with beryl and cornelian as secondary stones to guard the wearer against evil omens and passions. Virgo, the Virgin, is their sign of the Zodiac.

September Mascots

Those born in September are privileged to wear the sapphire as a mascot to ensure serenity of mind and avert dangers of fever and eyestrain.

It was supposed in the middle ages to dispel enchantments, ensure the favour of superiors, and render the influence of enemies powerless. It is the emblem of truth and constancy. Saturn and Venus are the guardian planets. Stability of character the personal inheritance, and Libra, the Scales, the astrological sign for those born in this month.

October Mascots

Those born in this month are destined to great strength of nature and extremes of material conditions. An opal is their talisman against the evils which may beset them but which will be overcome by the combined strength of their mascot, their ruling planets, Jupiter and Mars, and the steadfastness of their own natures. They frequently present a changeable and moody surface character just as the opal presents many changes of colour, but beneath this lies the tenacity of purpose with which they are endowed by their astrological sign, Scorpio, the Scorpion, and they usually attain their ends. Lodestone and adamant are their secondary birth stones.

November Mascots

The golden topaz is the birth stone for those whose birthday is in November, as it is supposed to preserve both friendship and love in all truth and sincerity. The ancients believed that, if set in gold and worn upon the neck or left arm, it averted evil influences and gave courage, wit and personal safety to its wearer. Jupiter, Mercury and the Sun are all influential planets to the November born, and their secondary birth stones are jade and the carbuncle. Sagittarius, the Archer, is their astrological sign, endowing them with wit, keenness of vision and accuracy of judgement.

December Mascots

Those born in this month are fortunate in claiming the turquoise for their month stone.

> " If you will wear a turquoise blue,
> Success will crown whate'er you do,"

promises an old rhyme, but it goes on to say that the mascot must be a gift to possess these powers, not a bought jewel. It will, when given by a true friend, change colour when the wearer is threatened by illness or danger, taking to itself the evils it averts from its owner. Saturn is the ruling planet for this month and Capricorn the Zodiacal sign, while pearl and chalcedony are the secondary birth stones, the whole ensuring purity, amiability and peace of heart to the December born wearer.

SECTION V

YOUR FORTUNE IN THE TEA-CUP

MANY interesting matters are discussed over a " cup of tea," and more than a few are satisfactorily settled, frequently through the indications of fortune dictated by the mystic shapes left by the tea-leaves in the cups ; for as " straws show which way the wind blows," so do the small indications of Fate often show the inclinations of the minds that read or hear them. Coffee-grounds can be used but are less apt to throw themselves into interesting figures than tea-leaves, and so are more seldom employed. The method is as " old as the hills " and simplicity itself, for much depends on the powers of the individual reader to visualise shapes and memorise their meanings.

The tea-cup to be read should be emptied of all but a few drops of tea at the bottom of the cup. The person whose fortune is to be read must then swing the cup round three times by the handle in the direction taken by the hands of a clock. This shakes and spreads the leaves well over the cup, which should then be turned upside down for a few moments to drain away the moisture. The divination is now done by means of symbolism, a method which has been used from the days when Egyptian hieroglyphics formed the basis of language. Notice should be taken not only of the forms and shapes inside the cup, but their position with regard to the handle and bottom of the cup. Also, the various shapes should be taken together in a comprehensive reading, as unfortunate indications will then be balanced by good ones or confirmed by other signs as the case may be. When the balance between good and bad signs is about equal, it usually means a choice of ways and must be regarded as a warning to the one whose cup is read, to walk warily and choose only good and trodden ways in life, lest evil befall.

Where there is any difficulty in determining whether the

figures to be seen are male or female, the darker leaves represent male, and the lighter, female figures ; but if the shape is definite enough to be judged by dress or feature, then light leaves indicate blonde colouring, and dark leaves, brunette. The handle of the cup represents the home, and the brim of the cup the immediate future. For instance, should the shape of a letter be seen on the brim, just above the handle of the cup, the reader will say, " A letter is coming to your house ; it is even now in the post " ; but should the shape of the letter be seen at a little distance from the handle, the reader announces, " You will receive a letter soon." Leaves at the bottom of the cup are less fortunate than those on the sides, and also less immediate in point of occurrence.

Leaves to the left of the handle represent past events or neglected opportunities, while those to the right of the handle can be interpreted as present and future good fortune, unless very thick and cloudy.

When the leaves form uneven or serpentine lines, these may be taken as roads, rivers or railways, according to other signs. If the shapes are surrounded by small dots, a sum of money gained by the meaning of the shape so seen, is indicated. Definite lines show a straight course to be taken, broken or wavy ones signify indecision or a difficult choice ahead. Indeterminate shapes, full of dashes, show that there are enterprises afloat which need time for development. Curves or circles signify completed work or actions, while a clearly cut circle, enclosing a cross, is a sign of a hospital or even imprisonment for the one whose cup is read, unless there is an initial close to the shape, when this will indicate the name of the person to be thus detained.

Initials signify acquaintances if seen at the sides of the cup, relations if seen close to the handle, enemies if shown at the bottom of the cup.

The Fortune Teller is often asked whether the initials seen are those of the Christian names or surnames of acquaintances, to which it must be answered that they are the initials of the names by which the one whose cup is read knows them best. For instance, should that person be interested in a friend whose surname begins with a B, but whom she knows by a pet name beginning with C, it is the initial C which is likely to be seen in the tea-cup, not B, though the initial B might well stand for the same person in the cup of one who does not know or use B's pet name.

A FEW EXAMPLES AND DELINEATIONS

A common sign of good luck is the horse-shoe, though its meaning varies according to its position. It is not generally known that a horse-shoe only brings luck when hung the right way up, that is, with the opening upwards, cup-like, so as to contain the good luck—not downward, or it may drop out. So also the tea-cup symbol must be in the right position. Near the top of the cup it indicates good fortune coming soon ; on the right of the handle it is not far off ; opposite the handle it is delayed but you will get it eventually ; at the bottom of the cup it is yours by right, but enemies are preventing it from reaching you. Should dots surround the horse-shoe, the nature of the good fortune is money ; a heart shape near it indicates success in love ; a cross close to it indicates property coming to you through a death ; but if the horse-shoe is turned upside down and to the left of the handle, you have had excellent chances of good fortune but have thrown them away.

Another sign frequently seen is a boat shape, which does not always indicate a journey by water to be taken by the one whose cup is read. Should an initial be seen near it, the journey will be taken by a friend whose name begins with that initial, probably a journey from across the water to see you. Birds flying above a boat indicate news from over the water, and a serpent near the boat, danger by water. Straight lines near the boat indicate escape from the danger, however, and show that the sign is only a warning of possible danger to the incautious.

A sword is the sign of an enemy, and jewellery, such as bracelets or brooches, represent admirers, unless broken, when they represent the loss of a devoted lover.

These are only a few of the signs or indications to be seen in the tea-cup. Many more signs and interpretations are to be found in a companion volume, entitled *Tea-Cup Fortune-Telling*